W9-BWZ-900

COMMUNISM

End of the Monolith?

edited by EVELYN GELLER

THE REFERENCE SHELF

Volume 50   Number 3

THE H. W. WILSON COMPANY

New York   1978

THE REFERENCE SHELF

The books in this series contain reprints of articles, excerpts from books, and addresses on current issues and social trends in the United States and other countries. There are six separately bound numbers in each volume, all of which are generally published in the same calendar year. One number is a collection of recent speeches; each of the others is devoted to a single subject and gives background information and discussion from various points of view, concluding with a comprehensive bibliography. Books in the series may be purchased individually or on subscription.

Library of Congress Cataloging in Publication Data

Main entry under title:

Communism.
    (The Reference shelf ; v. 50, no. 3)
    Bibliography: p.
    1. Communism—1945—   —Addresses, essays,
lectures. I. Geller, Evelyn. II. Series.
HX44.C642   335.43′09′047   78-13453
ISBN 0-8242-0624-X

PRINTED IN THE UNITED STATES OF AMERICA

PREFACE

The three and a half decades since the Second World War have witnessed a sharp increase in the number and variety of Communist countries across the world. The monolithic Cold War image of the 1950s, in which "free" and "Communist" blocs of nations confronted each other across an Iron Curtain, has been radically changed.

National communism is a term often used loosely to designate the diversity of Communist rule. It suggests that the doctrine and practice of communism may vary country by country and that these variations stem from national need and cultural tradition. It also hints that this diversity may include national autonomy—that is, independence, or even repudiation of the USSR as a center of leadership. And it implies that national interests and sentiments are potent forces cross-cutting the traditional international ideology of communism.

National communism emerged soon after World War II, when in 1948 Marshal Tito (Josip Broz), who had been an ardent supporter of Stalin, successfully asserted Yugoslavia's independence of Soviet control. In 1960 Mao Tse-tung repeated that pattern, attacking Soviet ideology as "revisionist" (not adequately orthodox in the Marxist-Leninist sense) and initiating the Sino-Soviet conflict that persists to this day. Moreover, the ruthlessly suppressed revolts in Hungary (1956) and Czechoslovakia (1968) gave additional evidence that the solidarity of the Communist bloc required the constant threat of USSR force. As late as March 1978, Tito visited Washington, seeking reassurance from President Jimmy Carter of support of his autonomy or "nonalignment" in relation to the USSR and urging stronger economic ties with the United States, despite the fact that his closest economic ties were by then with the USSR. (*U.S. News & World Report*, March 22, 1978)

3

Tito and Mao, however, pursued different kinds of nonalignment. Tito's regime has been described by a New York *Times* correspondent as a "unique brand of communism that he has used to challenge both the Soviet-style dictatorships of East Europe and the democracies of the West" (David Andelman, March 5, 1978). Mao, in 1959 and 1960, repudiated Khrushchev for having denounced Stalin, made peace with Tito, permitted peaceful paths to socialism, and taken an insufficiently militant line against imperialism. Mao's Third-World stance, based on anticolonialism, seemed more sharply opposed to both East and West.

Although nationalism in developing countries did not necessarily take a Socialist direction, it sometimes merged with communism in a peculiarly potent fusion. In the face of foreign domination rather than a ruling class, class consciousness was transmuted into patriotism and class conflict into "national liberation"—revolution against colonial dominion. National liberation movements—in Cuba and Algeria, among other countries—complicated the Cold War picture, setting industrial and developing countries against each other.

In the 1960s, Vietnam was the main setting of the national-liberation struggle. In the mid-1970s, in the midst of so-called détente, strategically located, resource-rich Angola became the scene of a war of national liberation in which the United States, the USSR, China, Cuba, South Africa, and Zaïre (formerly the Democratic Republic of Congo), all had a financial or military investment. While Congress eschewed involvement in "another Vietnam," in early 1978 the dispute between Ethiopia and Somalia, another strategic area, raised the same specter of USSR-led intervention and victory—this time in the Horn of Africa—prompting President Jimmy Carter's address on defense policy and policy toward the USSR.

The most recent variant of national communism has been "Eurocommunism"—the name now given to the ideology of Communist parties functioning openly and peacefully in capitalist societies with democratic political institutions.

Neither new nor uniquely or characteristically Western European (it existed in Chile with Allende and exists in Japan—but does not characterize Portugal's hard-line Communist party), Eurocommunism has developed its own identity and political strength, especially in Italy. Its twin platform is independence of Moscow and commitment to political democracy, including the right of dissent, multiparty systems, and displacement through the electoral process. Holding their own summit meeting in Madrid in March 1977, the three Eurocommunist leaders—Georges Marchais of France, Enrico Berlinguer of Italy, and Santiago Carrillo of Spain—declared their intent to provide a new center of international leadership.

The emergence of Eurocommunism has, however, met with skepticism from many sides. J. O. Goldsborough (*Foreign Affairs*, July 1977) describes the movement as strategically "unsettling," hence alarming to both the United States and the Soviet Union. In many respects the USSR is suspicious of the independence of Eurocommunist parties, whereas the United States distrusts any Communist party that is in regular contact with the USSR. In hard fact, the French Socialist-Communist coalition, beset with disagreement, lost to the center parties in the March 1978 elections, and in Italy, the shaky Communist-Christian Democratic coalition government has been under severe, often violent, attack by radical and terrorist Communists as a bourgeois accommodation—an attack culminating in the spring of 1978 in the kidnapping and assassination of the Christian Democratic leader Aldo Moro, a former premier who might have become president.

How much has the world view of the 1950s changed, and what elements remain, or recur, of that perspective? What are the varieties of national communism? What kinds of regimes do wars of national liberation produce? How credible are the claims of Eurocommunists? What are their ties to Moscow, and what are the potential effects of their doctrines? How does their parliamentary communism differ from socialism and from radical, Maoist communism? Finally, how do the large world powers perceive these changes?

These are the issues to which this volume is addressed. Section I explores the varieties of national communism and the history behind what one author calls communism's "crisis of authority." Section II treats the regimes in Vietnam and Angola, then Somalia's shifts in allegiance, as exemplifying some Third-World tensions. Section III, on the Western Hemisphere, describes the Cuban regime and the meaning for Marxists of Chile's foiled attempt at socialism.

Section IV turns to Eurocommunism, its background, present relationships, and potential influence in Western and Eastern Europe. Section V focuses on Italy as best exemplifying the problems of Eurocommunism. Section VI places national communism in the larger context of world policy.

The editor thanks the authors and publishers who granted permission to reprint the selections in this volume.

EVELYN GELLER

June 1978

CONTENTS

III. The Western Hemisphere

IV. Eurocommunism

V. Italy: A Case Study

VI. The Superpowers: Détente and Defense

I. VARIETIES OF NATIONAL COMMUNISM

EDITOR'S INTRODUCTION

As the number of Communist countries in the world has proliferated, so has their variety—a variety sometimes clumsily caught up in the term *national communism*. In contrast to the two-bloc stereotype of the Cold War, the term suggests both differences among Communist regimes stemming from differing national traditions and ideologies and independence of Soviet control. But the term has been applied to established one-party regimes, revolutionary cadres leading wars of national liberation, multiparty systems of capitalist democracies, and guerrilla movements, all showing varying degrees of adherence to USSR dictates.

Before objects can be compared, they must be described in comparable terms. The first two articles in this section, both from *U.S. News & World Report*, suggest the complex array of factors essential to even a cursory survey. In an ever-changing situation, the articles are less important for the facts they set down than for the range of factors they incorporate. The first selection summarizes the global balance of Communist influences as it existed recently in terms of regimes, parties, and movements and of their degree of power and mode of control. The second article outlines the ways in which even loyal Communist regimes can differ internally: in matters of permissible dissent, religious freedom, private production and property, consumer orientation, industrialization, foreign investment, trade with capitalistic countries, and agreement or conflict with the Soviet Union.

The third article, written by Daniel Seligman for *Fortune*, traces communism's "crisis of authority" from Stalin's death in 1953 through the efforts the USSR has made to keep communism international, unified, and Moscow-led.

It describes the early independence of Yugoslavia and Albania, Khrushchev's and Brezhnev's efforts to maintain control while endorsing freedom, Mao's defection, the long history of Eurocommunism, and differences among Eurocommunist countries.

The fourth article, by James Burnham, from *National Review*, discusses the country in which national communism was born, Yugoslavia. Tito's early excommunication by Stalin brought Yugoslavia into contact with the West, and this exposure, as well as cultural tradition, may explain some of the differences in its brand of communism: allowance for a small private sector, an apparent freedom of expression and religion, open economic and cultural relationships with the West—all within a structure of state ownership. (For a critique of the Yugoslavian regime, the old but well-known study *The New Class*, by Milovan Djilas, is a classic; for a discussion of unique aspects of the regime, see Dennison I. Rusinow's "Marxism, Belgrade Style," in Bertsch and Ganschow's *Comparative Communism*.)

Finally, a brief article discusses limited diversity within the East European monolith itself: different attitudes toward consumer needs, responses to worker unrest, and sources of tension that could produce further change.

WORLD COMMUNISM 1976: A PRECARIOUS BALANCE [1]

Reprinted from *U.S. News & World Report*.

The strong gains made by the Communist party in Italy's [1976] national elections focus fresh attention on the fortunes of "home grown" Communist movements. . . .

How potent are Communist parties outside the Soviet Union, Eastern Europe, and China? Are they close to achieving power? Answers come from overseas bureaus of *U.S. News & World Report*:

[1] From "Where Communists Are Gaining and Losing—in Bids for Power: Global Survey." *U.S. News & World Report*. 81:26–8. Jl. 5, '76.

Europe: Rising Influence vs. Nagging Doubts

In Britain, the Communist party exercises political muscle far out of proportion to its punch at the ballot box.

There are no Communists in Parliament. Only six Communists are in local government bodies, down from 50 . . . [in 1973]. Yet the party has strong influence on policies of the ruling Labour government. Here's how it works:

Of the 1.25 million members of the Engineering Workers Union, only 2,500 are Communists. But they occupy 16 of the 52 seats on the union's national committee. Fifteen of 39 members of the national executive of the Transport and General Workers Union, Britain's largest, also are Communists. With the Engineers, the TGWU controls 40 percent of the votes at Labour party conferences.

Explains Bert Ramelson, the party's industrial organizer:

The Communist party is rooted in industry. It's hard to find an important enterprise anywhere in Britain where there are stewards and convenors [shop-floor organizers] who are not Communists. Pressure comes from below.

Links between the party and the Labour government are reinforced by 70 to 80 Labourites in Parliament who are considered left-wingers and close to the Communists.

But the party's membership has declined to 29,000 since 1974. Its share of the vote in February 1974 elections dropped to just .06 percent of the total vote.

To rebuild its strength, British Communists promise to uphold the nation's traditional liberties, including free political parties and independence of labor unions. And they blame Moscow's policies—and conditions inside the Soviet Union—for their own waning appeal.

France's Communists are handicapped by two built-in weaknesses: The French man on the street distrusts them, and workers are more interested in money than ideology.

The party leans toward western-style democracy, attacks repression in Russia and claims to have abandoned the Leninist goal of the "dictatorship of the proletariat."

It claims 500,000 members, which would make it the

second largest Communist party in the non-Communist world next to Italy's. Although some experts argue that membership is closer to 300,000, the party received more than one fifth of the 16 million votes cast in 1973 elections and has 74 of the 490 seats in the National Assembly.

Nevertheless, the French still do not consider the Communists to be entirely responsible.

According to public-opinion polls, nearly half the French would not oppose Communist participation in the government. But most object to the party's being given dominant power. The French seem to believe that once in the saddle the Communists never would dismount.

Adding to the party's problems, most French workers are far more interested in keeping their jobs than in battling their employers or the government. Despite control of France's largest trade union, the party has been unable to make the union a militant force on behalf of communism.

Heartened by results of the Italian election, the party is pushing hard what it calls "socialism with a human face," trying to convince the French that it advocates vigorous nationalism free of Soviet direction.

But in the words of the conservative newspaper *Le Figaro:* "The Communist party, all smiles, is not a box-office success. The party's totalitarian image still gives cause for second thoughts."

Italy's 1.7 million Communists lost a skirmish in the June ... [1976] elections. . . .

The outlook now is for the party to push ahead with its strategy of "creeping compromise" at lower levels throughout the country. This strategy calls for entering coalitions wherever possible, giving the Italian people the impression of a party which cooperates with its opposition in the name of unity and democracy.

Communist strength is rooted among industrial workers. But the party also has a large following among students and intellectuals, in the film and artistic communities, and among journalists. A growing segment of the middle class supports the party, even though large numbers of Italians—

apparently heeding warnings of the anti-Communist Roman Catholic Church—switched their support from small parties to the Christian Democrats.

The Spanish Communist Party is illegal at home and is forced to work underground from its headquarters in Paris. [The party has recently been legalized.—Ed.]

. . . It enjoys strong support among Spanish workers and intellectuals and is capable at any time of provoking extensive social turmoil through strikes and demonstrations.

The party boasts it might get from 15 to 20 percent of the vote if allowed to participate in free elections.

Portugal's Communists hew faithfully to Moscow's line and are contemptuous of other parties in Western Europe.

Their leader, Alvaro Cunhal, sticks to his goal of establishing a "dictatorship of the proletariat." [For reactions to Cunhal, see "A Crisis of Authority," by Daniel Seligman, below in this section.]

Although the party has a total membership of 120,000, its popular base is fairly narrow—organized industrial workers and farm workers on big estates close to and south of Lisbon. It is tightly knit and highly disciplined. But most experts agree it is far too rigid to have much chance any time soon of taking power—or sharing it—at the national level.

In Greece, Communists are split into four groups—three of them legalized after the military junta was thrown out of office in 1974. They use such pocketbook issues as unemployment and inflation to increase their strength in the labor unions and student bodies.

Scandinavia: Haves and Have-Nots

Sweden . . . [has been a] center of European attention. . . . The Communists suffer from internal splits. The majority, as in France, favors a national brand of communism with a "human face." A tough minority want to follow Moscow's dictates. The minority's greatest strength is found among manual workers who dislike the growing influence of party "intellectuals"—those who dare to criticize the Kremlin.

In Norway, the Communists are completely shut out of parliament, and in Denmark they . . . [held] only 7 of 179 seats [in 1976].

In Finland, however, the Communists . . . [have been] the second largest party, trailing only the Social Democrats. . . . [In 1976] they got 19 percent of the votes and 40 seats in the 200-seat parliament—down slightly from their peak strength in the 1950s. They share power in a coalition government with four other parties and . . . [in 1976 held] 4 of 18 cabinet posts.

Iceland's Communist-dominated People's Alliance opposes NATO and American forces on the island and wants the nation to be neutral and unarmed. The Alliance captured 11 of 60 seats in parliament in 1974 elections with 18.3 percent of total votes cast.

Asia: From Government to Underground

Japan's Communist party is dynamic and increasingly popular. But it is a long way from taking political power in an essentially conservative nation.

The party . . . [had] 370,000 members [in 1976] and is one of the largest in the non-Communist world. . . . It . . . [has taken] 10.5 percent of the vote and close to 10 percent of the seats in both houses of the Diet. Communists also hold more than 3,000 seats in local governments.

One measure of the party's broad appeal: The Communist newspaper *Akahata*—Red Flag—sells 650,000 copies each weekday and 2.4 million every Sunday in a nation of 110 million people.

The Communists in Japan say they would not nationalize even large industries immediately—but would "someday"—should they ever form a national government. And if voted out of office, they promise to respect the voters' decision.

Other assurances include a pledge to retain the Emperor system, freedom of religion and the country's democratic constitution. The party asserts its independence from both

Moscow and Peking and insists there should be no "international center of Communism."

Sri Lanka is an exception to the party's failure in Asia to gain a firm foothold in governments—outside China and Communist-led Indo-China.

The Prime Minister, Mrs. Sirimavo Bandaranaike, has both the pro-Soviet Communist party and the Trotskyist LSSP (Ceylon Equal Society party) in her government. Together, the two parties have 25 of 157 seats in the legislature.

The Trotskyites control the Ceylon Federation of Labor and are supported by two unions of government employees. But the two parties together have a total membership of only about 3,000 in a population of 12.8 million.

India's various Communist factions total about 200,000 members in a nation of nearly 600 million. [In 1976] there . . . [were] 49 Communists in the 521-seat legislature and well over 100 in various state assemblies.

Aside from pro-Maoist groups, the Communists generally support Prime Minister Indira Gandhi and her ruling Congress party. The pro-Soviet wing of the party denounces as "adventurists" and "counterrevolutionaries" all those who criticize Mrs. Gandhi. [Mrs. Gandhi and her Congress party were defeated in the 1977 elections.—Ed.]

In Pakistan, some journalists holding important editorial positions display strong Communist leanings. But Prime Minister Zulfikar Ali Bhutto brooks little opposition to his strongman rule. The Pakistani Communist party has negligible membership and almost no appeal among the people. [Bhutto was overthrown by a military coup in July 1977. —Ed.]

In Bangladesh, the now-independent former province of Eastern Pakistan, the pro-Soviet Communist party has to contend with at least five Maoist groups that find more favor with the revolutionary young.

In the Philippines, pro-Soviet and pro-Peking Communists have been driven underground by President Ferdinand Marcos. The pro-Peking group is more active and has sought common cause with Moslem rebels in Mindanao and other southern islands. But the Moslem movement there is essentially a non-Communist revolt against Christian landowners.

Indonesia's once-powerful Communist party, the oldest in Asia, has never recovered from its unsuccessful coup attempt in 1965. Communists still undertake small-scale guerrilla activity in Kalimantan, formerly Borneo, but the Indonesian military has had no trouble coping with them.

Malaysian Communists, mostly Chinese, go in for ambushes and hit-and-run attacks. They have stepped up their assaults since the US withdrawal from Vietnam—and apparently are getting weapons smuggled in from Indo-China.

Thailand's northeastern sector is kept in constant ferment by several thousand Communist guerrillas with the help of some aid provided from Communist-run Laos. Another Communist target: labor unions and students in Bangkok.

Burma's Communist underground has about 7,000 men bearing arms. Government troops in the northern part of the country next door to China—which provides some support to the guerrillas—have a hard time holding their own.

Africa: Soviets Come A-wooing

There are no formally organized Communist parties anywhere in black Africa. Yet at least nine countries have left-wing, one-party governments that practice Marxism in one form or another.

Somalia calls its state ideology "scientific socialism." [For Somalia's switch, see "Somalia: Changing of the Guard," below in Section II.]

Tanzania has "African socialism." Of the 103 delegations that attended the twenty-fifth Soviet Communist party congress . . . [in 1976], 11 were from black African nations: Angola, Congo, Guinea, Guinea-Bissau, Malagasy Republic, Mozambique, Namibia, Rhodesia, Senegal, Somalia and Tanzania, plus the outlawed South African Communist party.

The Soviet Union courts the military governments of

Nigeria and Uganda as assiduously as it woos left-wing regimes. [In 1976] Soviet military aid . . . [was] going to 11 African countries, according to one estimate, and 19 African states . . . [had] Russian military advisers instructing their armed forces.

Latin America: Hard Row to Hoe

Communist parties are illegal in much of Latin America.

Chile and Uruguay . . . [have been] rewriting their constitutions to outlaw any form of Marxism.

In Brazil, captured Communists are put on trial after "interrogation" that one authority calls "worse than the prison sentence."

Colombian and Venezuelan Communists are allowed to campaign, but they receive little support from the voters.

Guyana's Prime Minister Forbes Burnham follows policies similar to those of Tito's Yugoslavia and says he wants to create a Marxist-Leninist society. His chief opposition, the People's Progressive party led by Cheddi Jagan, . . . announced its "critical" support for the government [in 1976].

Jamaica's Prime Minister Michael Manley has moved closer to Communist Cuba. He describes his program as "democratic socialism" and promises to preserve Jamaica's parliamentary system, its free press and individual rights.

Peru's acquisition of Soviet arms beginning in 1973 and the presence of Russians and Cubans in the country have raised concern among neighboring nations.

However, experts on Latin America spot no signs of rising Communist influence from the outside. The small Communist party of Peru is split into rival pro-Soviet and Maoist factions. Its main strength lies in labor unions.

In Mexico, Communist and radical Marxist parties are legal but are small and weak.

The Mexican Communist party has an estimated 5,000 members and follows a line relatively independent of Moscow. The Popular Socialist party claims about 75,000 members and has refrained from violence to achieve its goals.

Most terrorism in Mexico is carried out by the radical "23rd of September Communist League," which is disavowed by the official Communist party.

In Panama, all political parties, including the Communists, have been banned since the 1968 military coup.

Panama's strongman, General Omar Torrijos Herrera, emphasized on his return from a visit to Cuba early . . . [in 1976] that Havana had chosen its road to social progress, but that Panama had decided to take another route. "Today," he said, "Panama's economy is one of the prime examples of the free-enterprise system in Latin America."

Elsewhere

Elsewhere around the world, Communist parties pack little or no punch in most countries.

A major exception is Australia where three main Communist groups, totaling about six thousand members, wield strong influence within the trade-union movement.

But in Canada, the party's two thousand members are rejected by the Left and assailed by more radical Maoists and Trotskyites as relics of the past. In West Germany, Switzerland, and Austria, the party's prestige is insignificant.

Nevertheless, whether Communists are strong, weak, even outlawed, governments have learned from bitter experience that the party cannot be ignored. They have learned that Communist leaders are determined to grab power—whether through democratic processes or violent overthrow of established institutions.

CRACKS IN THE MONOLITH [2]

Reprinted from *U.S. News & World Report*

Around the world today, 1.3 billion people—nearly one third of earth's total population—live in 16 countries ruled by Communists.

The numbers are awesome. They create in the popular

[2] From "What's Causing the Cracks in the Communist Monolith?" *U.S. News & World Report.* 81:66–8. N. 1, '76.

imagination the picture of a united and monolithic force.
. . . Yet, more and more, facts are turning up a far different
picture. . . .

A Yugoslav enjoys far more freedom—to travel and read
foreign books, even to criticize his government—than do the
Rumanians or the Vietnamese. Albanians and North Ko-
reans have few personal liberties.

None of the Communist nations are police states in the
Stalinist sense of the midnight knock at the door. Yet fear
of being thrown into jail, a "re-education" camp, or an insane asylum is never very far from the minds of those who
disagree with the system under which they live.

In some Communist countries, one may practice religion
without much official hindrance. In others, public worship
is under tight wraps.

Some Communist governments invite foreign investment; others ban it entirely. A few permit private enterprise
and allow farmers to own their land. Elsewhere everything
is nationalized, yet moonlighting for profit is widespread. . . .
Governments take different directions in economic planning and development, even while claiming to be socialist-
oriented.

Deeply ingrained nationalism explains why many Communist regimes decline guidance from either Moscow or
Peking. . . . [There follows] a close look at the world Communist movement—how it is developing and where it is
heading . . . [opinions of] top specialists in the United States
and other countries. . . .

Policies Toward Religious Freedom

The Soviet Union's constitution guarantees freedom of
worship, yet the government forbids religious education and
from time to time sponsors antireligion campaigns. But after
six decades of stern atheistic rule, the various religions still
have followers.

Albania, one of the most radical Communist countries,
abolished all religious institutions in 1967 and proclaimed
itself "the first atheist state in the world."

Rumania has abolished Roman Catholic orders and put the clergy on its payroll. East Germany completely controls the Federation of Evangelical Churches. Hungary eased pressure on the Catholic church in 1964, but priests were required to swear loyalty to the government.

In Poland, 95 percent of the people are practicing Catholics. Under its stubborn primate, Stefan Cardinal Wyszynski, the church has the only truly independent congregation in the Communist world. In Yugoslavia's relatively free atmosphere, religion holds its own. Yet there are signs that President Tito is moving to restrict religious freedom because of fear that ethnic separatists might exploit the situation.

In China, western faiths that have never struck deep or widespread roots are tolerated within narrow limits.

Political Rights

Some of the Communist nations call themselves "democratic republics" or "people's republics." In fact, in all of the countries, authority is centralized in the Communist party. Political opposition exists only inside the party, although non-Communist puppet parties survive in Poland, Bulgaria and East Germany. The press and radio are tightly controlled. Secret police make sure there is no deviation from major policy lines.

In the Soviet Union, dissidents are subject to peremptory arrest, sham trials, stints in insane asylums or harsh labor camps and deportation. The human-rights group, Amnesty International, accuses the Soviet regime of holding ten thousand political and religious prisoners.

Rumania is moderate in its foreign policy and eager for contacts with the West but runs one of the strictest internal regimes in the Communist world.

Isolated Albania is a vast prison. And little real freedom exists in Czechoslovakia, Bulgaria, Outer Mongolia, China, North Korea, Vietnam, Laos and Cambodia. East Germany has the Wall to keep people in and ideas out.

In contrast, Poland and Hungary are considered enlightened by Communist standards. Yugoslavia comes closest to granting its people substantial freedoms—including easy access to western ideas. Yet many dissidents and nationalists have been jailed in recent years.

Elites and Masses

Communists everywhere pay lip service to Karl Marx's concept of the Communist society: "From each according to his abilities, to each according to his needs." In practice, the classless society is nowhere in sight. Every Communist country develops a new ruling elite that holds power and also enjoys substantial material privileges. Throughout the Communist world the basic Marxist tenet of equality is mocked by high-living leaders and bureaucrats.

Only in China—and its [former] imitator, Albania—has there been any real attempt to establish a semblance of equality among all divisions of society. And even in China, party cadres dress and live better than the masses.

In Russia, privileged hierarchies are clearly defined in the Communist party, the government, the scientific community and in other areas. Top officials get lavish houses, cottages in the countryside, cars and trips abroad.

In stark contrast, the workers in most Communist countries are at the foot of the economic ladder. Agricultural laborers, especially, are victims of wage discrimination.

Average monthly wages for industrial workers run from a high of $400 in East Germany to a low of $30 in China. With food, housing, education and medical care heavily subsidized by the regimes, workers survive and in some countries even save a little. . . . Any serious depletion of their buying power through price hikes precipitates the kind of unrest that rocked Poland . . . [in June 1975]. . . .

Private Enterprise

[There are, however,] those who operate private businesses in some Communist countries.

In Poland, for instance, about 400,000 workers were

in private enterprise in 1975—driving cabs, running restaurants and small shops. Yugoslavia also permits private
enterprise—provided an employer does not have more than
five persons on his payroll.

In the Soviet Union, all business is owned and run by
the state, and even individual craftsmen are forbidden to
hire help. Yet moonlighting, accompanied by illegal use of
government tools and supplies in private deals, and an
astoundingly lucrative black market are realities of life.

Scandals are frequently mentioned in the Soviet press.
Some recent examples: members of an Armenian collective
farm letting their organization go to ruin while making
money growing high-priced flowers; officials of a sugar refinery using the plant's materials to make grave markers
and religious statues; store managers and clerks buying up
whole consignments of goods to resell in "flea markets."

Agriculture: Collective and Private

All Communist governments tried at one time or another to abolish private ownership of land and force people
into state or collective farms.

Stalin liquidated an entire class of people, the kulaks
or prosperous farmers. The Chinese Communists were
equally ruthless with landlords . . . [in order] to meet one
objective—forced agricultural output—to provide capital
for rapid industrialization.

In the Soviet Union, almost the entire agricultural
sector is now run by the state through 29,600 collective
farms and 17,700 state farms. Yet private farming survives
on "backyard plots." Although these plots total no more
than 4 percent of the Soviet Union's farm acreage, they produce 64 percent of the potato crop, 53 percent of all vegetables, 41 percent of the eggs and 22 percent of all meat
and milk.

China's more than 800 million people get almost all of
their food from 50,000 communes or supercollectives. State
farms account for only 10 percent of the arable land. Mem-

bers of the communes are permitted to grow fruit and vegetables on tiny, individual plots, or raise a few chickens or a
pig.

In Poland and Yugoslavia, more than 80 percent of all
the farmland is privately owned and highly productive.

Cuba's 180,000 private farms are to be phased out under
new economic plans.

Industrial Development and Foreign Enterprise

In recent years, Communist governments have started
turning to the capitalist countries for modern plants and
sophisticated technology. The Soviet Union and China
have the resources to meet most of the costs of these expensive imports. But even Russia is opening its doors
slightly to foreign firms willing to participate in new self-
liquidating ventures. Payment is made in the product of
an enterprise.

Others, unable to pay their bills, must borrow or even
seek foreign investment in certain sectors of their economies. In fact, the total foreign debts of Russia and the
Eastern European bloc may hit 40 billion dollars this year
—a sum that worries western bankers and governments.

Yugoslavia, Poland, Rumania, and Hungary want foreign capital and toy with the idea of joint ventures. It's
the one way they can finance certain types of industry or
import technology.

Yugoslavia permits a foreign investor to own 49 percent of an enterprise, and several American firms have developed substantial stakes there. Hungary prefers cooperative agreements, of which some one thousand have been
signed with western firms. Rumania tries to lure investors
with promises of guaranteed profits. Bucharest has an Intercontinental Hotel, built and operated by Pan American World Airways but owned by the Rumanian government.

Poland's debts from rapid industrialization run between five and seven billion dollars. Now it is turning to

the West, urging foreigners to invest in small private businesses, with the understanding that some of the profits can be taken out of the country each year.

There is no single pattern governing industrial growth in the Communist world. The Soviet Union still assigns top priority to heavy industries, including weapons production, but is putting more and more capital into agriculture—with limited success.

China has had a remarkable growth rate for industry—averaging 8 to 10 percent over the last fifteen years. Now emphasis has shifted to light or intermediate industries, particularly those that back up the nation's all-out quest for a breakthrough in agriculture.

Conflict Among Communist Governments

The Communist world today is wracked by quarrels between governments, clashing national interests and disagreement over policies toward non-Communist countries.

China and the Soviet Union are such bitter foes that some observers consider their split to be irreparable. Sino-Soviet rivalry is a constant disruptive factor among other Communist nations.

Yugoslavia broke with Moscow nearly three decades ago and still insists on following its own totally independent foreign policy. It is a leader of the nonaligned countries. Another rebel against Soviet hegemony is tiny Albania. . . .

Soviet troops, used against Hungary in 1956 and Czechoslovakia in 1968, are still on hand to see that Eastern Europe stays in line. That threat, however, has not deterred Rumania. Bucharest openly asserts its independence, has sought close relations with the West and is the only Communist capital that has diplomatic ties with Israel.

Analysts warn that the disarray does not vitally affect the interdependence of the Communist nations, especially when they face an external threat. Says one observer: "The US should be wary of accepting Communist schisms as proof of serious weakness in the system until we learn to

differentiate between the ideological and practical reasons
for the various splits."

Others insist that nationalism has made such serious
inroads that the once proverbial cohesion of the Communist world has been lost. As one western observer puts it:

"They may be all Communists, but they are all nationalists as well."

A CRISIS OF AUTHORITY [3]

In the last few years, many thoughtful and educated
Americans have become aware of a gathering confusion in
their minds about the international Communist movement.
They are not even sure which parties around the world
should be thought of as Communist. Between 1919 and
1943, the Communist International served as a kind of
"accreditation bureau"; today, there just isn't any agreed-
on procedure for deciding which parties to count.

More important, an educated American today is somewhat blurry about what it is that Communists stand for.
Many Communists are no longer supporters of Soviet interests. The making of foreign policy in the People's Republic of China, for example, often seems to consist mainly
of a search for ways to *damage* Soviet interests.

The International "Movement": Party or Parties?

Most confusing of all is the fact that some of those "independent" parties are now caught up in still another
heresy: they reject the idea of one-party rule—or at least
say they do. In Italy, Spain, and Japan, for example, the
political and economic programs of the Communists are in
many respects similar to those of social-democratic parties.
While not forswearing "solidarity" with the Soviet Union,
these Communist parties have been critical of the more repressive features of Soviet life and insistent that these

[3] From article entitled "Communism's Crisis of Authority," by Daniel
Seligman, senior staff editor. *Fortune.* 93:92–5+. F. '76. Reprinted from the
February 1976 issue of Fortune magazine by special permission; © 1976 Time Inc.

would not be duplicated if they came to power themselves. All these parties say that they would respect civil liberties and would retire from office if the vote went against them.

The new diversity in the Communist world is a source of confusion to Communists themselves. While the history of their movement has featured endless disagreements about doctrine, it has always been an article of faith among Communists that they are enlisted in a common cause. Lenin, Stalin, Khrushchev, Brezhnev, Mao—each has had his own interpretation of Communist doctrine, but all have proudly proclaimed themselves to be internationalists.

There may well have been some genuine feeling behind a remark made by Leonid Brezhnev toward the end of the Twenty-fourth Congress of the Soviet Communist party in Moscow . . . [in 1971]: "While listening to the speeches of our foreign friends and brothers, we felt ever more strongly that we were an inalienable, integral part of the great international movement called upon to transform the world."

But if there is no longer agreement on Soviet leadership, or on the Soviet "model" as the ultimate objective of Communists everywhere, then the purposes of the international movement become most unclear. It is not overstating matters to suggest that the movement today suffers from a profound crisis of authority. The Soviet leaders have fought a long rearguard action to preserve some semblance of their authority over the movement, but they have not had many victories during the past two decades.

Roots of the Crisis

The roots of the crisis go back to Stalin's death. The source of his authority appears, in retrospect, to have been a kind of religious mystique: Stalin was revered as something akin to a god. In any case, Soviet authority over other Communist parties began to dissolve rapidly after his death, and when he was denounced by Khrushchev in the February 1956 "secret speech," the Communist world was transformed.

The invasion of Hungary in the fall of 1956 gave some

Communist parties outside the Soviet sphere an issue on which to break with the Russians. But even before Hungary, a few parties had served notice that things were different. In an interview after the secret speech, Palmiro Togliatti, the leader of the Italian Communists, insisted optimistically that there would still be "solidarity" among Communist parties.

However [he added] not only the need but also the desire for increasingly greater autonomy in judgments will undoubtedly come out of this; and this cannot help but benefit our movement. The internal political structure of the world Communist movement has changed today.

For some time after the secret speech, Khrushchev made an effort to preserve the idea that the Soviet party was the movement's natural leader. In November 1957, on the fortieth anniversary of the Russian Revolution, there was a conference in Moscow of twelve ruling Communist parties. The conference featured an extraordinary speech by Mao Tse-tung proclaiming that the Soviet party was "at the head of the Communist world movement." The speech came at a time when the Russians had just embarked on a major program of military aid to China, and it is possible that Mao's words were to some extent "purchased" by this aid; in any case, the Russians were plainly gratified by his formulation, which was accepted by the eleven other parties at the conference.

But the formulation did not have a very long life. By the spring of 1959, the Russians had torn up their military agreement with the Chinese, and by the summer they had cut back sharply on economic aid as well. In addition to the bitterness engendered by these cutbacks, there was an emerging ideological war between the two Communist powers in this period, with the Chinese pressing for a more militant line in the war against "imperialism."

Repudiation of the Leading Center

When Communist parties from all around the world met in Moscow in the fall of 1960, it speedily became obvious that there would be no unanimous agreement about the Russians being "at the head of" things. Soviet leadership was flatly disavowed by the Chinese delegates and their Albanian allies. [Since the death of Mao Tse-tung, Albania has become increasingly critical of Peking policies. —Ed.] The chairman of the Albanian party, Enver Hoxha, proclaimed his own party's independence with heavy sarcasm:

> The fact that Albania proceeds along the path of socialism and that it is a member of the socialist camp is not determined by you, Nikita Khrushchev. It does not depend on your wishes. This has been determined by the Albanian people, headed by their Workers' Party.

Anticipating the inevitable, Khrushchev himself proposed the abandonment of any wording that implied Soviet authority over the international movement.

Four years later, Khrushchev made an effort to retrieve his party's leadership position. He began trying to organize still another world conference of Communist parties, at which a leading Soviet role might be acknowledged and the Chinese assailed; and after endless delays and years of negotiation, the conference was finally held in June 1969 in Moscow. But this time the final document left the Russians even worse off: it declared that "there is no leading center of the international Communist movement." Ever since then, the Soviet rulers have in principle—and to a considerable extent in practice—accepted the proposition that all parties have equal status. [For further historical analysis, see Edward Crankshaw's article "Europe's Reds: Trouble for Moscow," in Section IV, below.]

The 1969 meeting, the last one held by the world movement, was a major turning point in the history of communism. Kevin Devlin, a Radio Free Europe analyst whose research reports are a gold mine of information about interparty affairs, summarized the results with a metaphor borrowed from church history. "Nikita Khrushchev set out to convene the Council of Trent," said Devlin, "and Leonid Brezhnev ended up with Vatican II." (*The Council of*

Trent, convened by the church in 1545-63, strengthened the doctrinal system of Catholicism in the face of the Protestant challenge.) [Vatican II was an ecumenical council called in 1962 by Pope John XXIII and reconvened in 1963, 1964, and 1965 by Pope Paul VI; it was oriented toward church renewal.—Ed.]

The last world conference of Communist parties, . . . a disaster for its Soviet sponsors, . . . proclaimed that "there is no leading center of the international Communist movement"—implying that all parties have equal status. The delegates, from seventy-five parties, met in St. George's Hall in the Great Kremlin Palace.

Different "Roads" to Socialism

The decline of Soviet leadership in the world movement has been matched by a decline of interest in the Soviet version of communism. The view that there are "different roads to socialism" first surfaced in the wake of Tito's 1948 break with Stalin, when the Yugoslav Communists argued that their unique history gave them the right to strike out in new directions. The view that there are different roads to socialism was soon taken up by most of the world's influential Communist parties. At the Twentieth Congress of the Soviet party in 1956, Khrushchev himself conceded the point.

To an outsider, the view that there are different roads to socialism might seem to be no more than a truism. In fact, as the Soviet leaders have gradually come to realize, the "different roads" really imply quite different kinds of socialism. Communism today is being offered in several different varieties, ranging from the totalitarian Chinese model to the "democratic" model.

Viewing the damage done by the idea of different roads to socialism, the Soviet leaders have to some extent welshed on Khrushchev's 1956 concession. The official Soviet line today represents an effort to have it both ways. The line is that, while the building of socialism will of course be affected by specific national differences, there remain some general and immutable requirements—presumably reflecting the Soviet experience. As Brezhnev put the case in his report to the Twenty-fourth Congress: "Successes in Socialist construction largely depend on the correct combination of the general and the nationally specific in social development." Unfortunately for the Russians, it seems most unlikely that any amount of theorizing about "the correct combination" can restore a unity of purpose to the international movement.

The extent of the disunity is strikingly evident in the Soviet government's prolonged effort . . . to organize a conference of European Communist parties. Considering their dismal prior record on the conference front, it might seem odd that the Russians would be voluntarily returning to action there. Yet, only a few years after the 1969 debacle, they were trying to organize a new conference. Their objective, furthermore, seems to have been a new *world* conference—i.e., one with essentially the same cast of characters that had just proved to be so difficult.

1973: Calls for a World Congress

Beginning around the summer of 1973, Communists concerned with interparty affairs began to pick up rumors that the Russians might press for a new world meeting. Toward the end of that year, the rumors were confirmed, although not by the Russians themselves. Herbert Mies, the head of the West German Communist party, called for a European conference that would set the stage for a worldwide one; a bit later, the Hungarian and Bulgarian parties issued calls of their own for a world conference. Since none of these "loyalist" parties could conceivably have acted without Soviet guidance, it was clear enough that Soviet Communists wanted the conference (but also clear that they did not yet want to commit their own prestige to it). Nor was there any mystery about their objectives: both the Hungarian and Bulgarian statements included attacks on the Chinese.

All during the first half of 1974, the Soviet leaders continued, somewhat coyly, to indicate their interest in a world conference. In April, Boris Ponomarev, the Central Committee's secretary in charge of relations with "nonruling" parties, made a speech indicating that the Soviet party was "ready to take new steps" to further the meeting that, he said, others were calling for. By this time, a few more loyalist spokesmen in the satellite regimes had indeed spoken out, as had a few parties in the western industrial world (including the US Communist party). But there was a rather deafening silence from the larger and more influential parties in the West, and the independent-minded Rumanian and Yugoslav parties had expressed misgivings about the idea.

The Rumanians in particular were troublesome. They said that they could not possibly attend a world conference unless two conditions were met. First, the conference could not issue any statement at all unless it was agreed to by every party present. Second, even this unanimously accepted final statement would not be binding on the participants. As Kevin Devlin observed, the essential illogic of the pair of demands could only be read as a sign of obstructionist intent.

A Pan-European Congress

Evidently discouraged by all the obstacles to a world conference, the Russians began concentrating on a Pan-European conference: one that would bring together the East European satellite parties, the East European dissidents (Rumania and Yugoslavia), and the West Europeans —a total of thirty parties. Aside from the fact that it would presumably be easier to organize, a Pan-European conference had some real attractions for the Russians.

One attraction, it may be presumed, lay in the simple fact that the western parties would be forced to reestablish their identification with the "people's democracies" of Eastern Europe. The West European parties were increasingly casting themselves as a kind of "democratic bloc" within the international movement, and had got into the

habit of holding meetings among themselves—meetings to
which the Russians were not invited and at which their
major concerns (e.g., China) were not discussed. Regional
meetings of these parties had been held in Rome in 1959,
Brussels in 1965, and Vienna in 1966; and . . . in January
1974 there had been another meeting at Brussels, where
nineteen parties gathered in an effort to establish a common position toward the European Economic Community.

There was nothing overtly anti-Soviet about any of these
meetings. But the widespread impression that they were
becoming institutionalized, combined with the fact that
they were dominated by parties talking about a parliamentary version of communism, must have left the Russians
feeling uneasy about them. A Pan-European conference
would at least oblige the "democratic" Communists to ac-
knowledge their kinship with Lenin's heirs in Eastern Europe.

A Role for Eurocommunists:
Soviet vs. European Versions

In addition, the Russians had some fairly specific assignments for the West European Communists, and a conference would be useful if it helped to clarify these. The assignments called for the parties to influence both public
opinion and government policy so as to further Soviet objectives in two major negotiations with the western democracies.

One was at the European security conference, where the
Russians were trying to gain formal recognition of the national boundaries established after World War II, while
making only minimal concessions on political and cultural
freedom in their sphere. The other was at the Vienna negotiations on balanced force reductions, where the Russians
were pressing for a definition of "balance" under which the
western powers would make proportionally greater reductions in their force levels. As Ponomarev put it at one of
the meetings devoted to planning the Pan-European party

conference, Communists should be for "the formation of an all-European antimilitary coalition of various social and political forces." [For Brezhnev's comments at the Pan-European conference, which was held in June 1976, see his address in Section VI below.—Ed.]

The West European parties themselves were somewhat ambivalent about the conference proposal. Most of them, it seems fair to say, had no real objections to the substance of those "assignments." And even in terms of electoral politics, all of them felt there were some advantages to associating themselves with Soviet communism. To repudiate it would leave them with no very coherent answer when asked to explain what they offered that was different from all those other parties on the Left. On the other hand, there were some obvious dangers to a conference. West European Communists could suffer heavy electoral losses in their own countries if the arrangements and final pronouncement made it appear that they were again taking orders from Moscow.

It is true that not all the parties were equally sensitive to these dangers. The small West German, Austrian, and Danish parties seemed delighted to take their guidance from Moscow. And the French Communist party, which despite its new democratic posture has retained a strong pro-Soviet orientation, had only minimal objections to the Soviet conference proposals. But the Italian party, which has generally been the leader of those Communists taking the parliamentary road, was giving the Russians a hard time every step of the way.

So was the Spanish party ([then] in exile), whose eagerness to be legalized in the post-Franco era gave it a special incentive to make clear its independence of the Russians. The Swedish, British, and Swiss parties were also emphatic about their unwillingness to participate in a conference that might be construed as a Soviet effort to regain control over the international movement. As things turned out, these concerns about Soviet control led most of the West Europeans—who were joined by the dissident Yugoslav and Rumanian parties—to insist on terms that would have made the conference quite meaningless.

Debates on an Agenda

The first preparatory meeting, i.e., to establish ground rules for the conference, was held in Warsaw in October 1974. Twenty-eight of the thirty parties attended. (The Dutch and Icelandic parties, which have generally declined to cooperate with other Communists in recent years, declined once again.) While the proceedings were, of course, closed to the press, enough appeared in Italian party publications within a few weeks to suggest some of the issues that had been raised.

Gian Carlo Pajetta, a senior official of the Italian party who has special responsibility for interparty affairs, made it clear in an interview that the Italians had ruled out any "anathemas" against the Chinese at the conference. The conference would deal with political issues but, said Pajetta, there could be no "straying into the ideological field"; in other words, no judgments could be passed on the basic position of any party.

The Italians also insisted, according to Pajetta's account, that the final conclusions of the conference would be worked out "through common consensus" (which sounded something like that Rumanian demand for a right of veto). Furthermore, there could be "no decisions which for some come, as it were, from outside, or which represent some kind of obligation to others" (which sounded much like the Rumanian demand that nothing be binding on anyone). Finally, the Italians had proposed that the European party conference be somehow combined with a series of meetings between Communists and other Socialist parties.

This last demand must have been especially exasperating to the Russians because it worked to undermine one of their major ideas in calling for the Pan-European conference—the idea that it was time to remind Europe's Communists of their Leninist heritage. Within a few months, furthermore, the Yugoslavs moved to implement the Italian demand.

They organized a conference in Belgrade—on the subject of relations between Europe and the less developed countries—and scheduled it for April 1975. Among those invited, along with all the Communist parties of Europe, were twenty-six Socialist and Social-Democratic parties. Among those who ultimately accepted were some members of the British Labor party and a delegation from the Portuguese Socialist party, which was, of course, then locked in combat with the Portuguese Communists (who declined to send anyone to Belgrade when they learned that the Socialists would be there).

The Warsaw preparatory meeting was followed by others in Budapest in December 1974 and in East Berlin in February 1975 and again in April. No one disclosed much about the first two of these, but reports from Yugoslavia and Italy made it clear that there was a major row at the second East Berlin meeting. It appears that the East German party, which was at this point carrying the ball for the Russians, prepared a draft document describing the arrangements for the Pan-European conference that had allegedly been agreed to. It also appears that the Yugoslavs and Italians vehemently denied that the draft represented what they had agreed to and flatly rejected it as unacceptable. At this point, after four preparatory meetings, each of them attended by a majority of the twenty-eight parties, there was a complete lack of agreement about the purpose and arrangements of the conference.

Compromise?

With the Pan-European conference in obvious trouble after the row about that East German draft, Pajetta made a trip to Moscow . . . [in May 1975] to see if there was any basis at all for agreement. He returned to Rome, not with an answer to this question, but with a new procedural approach. Instead of trying to plan the conference with an "editorial commission" representing all twenty-eight parties, the participants would turn things over to a more manageable group of eight. The group would have four members representing "loyalist" parties (those of the Soviet Union, East Germany, France, and Denmark) and four representing the dissident parties (those of Yugoslavia, Rumania, Italy, and Spain).

Beginning . . . [in July 1975] this group met repeatedly in an effort to reach agreement. By October, it appeared to have succeeded; or, more precisely, it appeared that the Russians had thrown in the towel and granted all the dissidents' demands. The full editorial commission reconvened that month, and after its meeting the Italian party paper *l'Unità* reported with satisfaction that the conference could now proceed on the basis of "agreement of all the parties," i.e., any party could veto anything. This meant, obviously, that the conference would not accomplish anything of real substance—but that was fine with the Italians. According to *l'Unità*, the full editorial commission would meet one more time, in November, to work out minor logistical details.

But it did not turn out that way. When the editorial commission met again in East Berlin, the dissident parties were greeted, to their astonishment, by a reassertion of some loyalist demands that had previously been abandoned. No outsider knows in any detail which demands were revived. It probably doesn't matter. What seems to have happened is that the Russians, taking a final look at the conference they had labored for two years to produce, decided it just wasn't worthwhile—that the conditions attached to it meant it couldn't possibly be an event Brezhnev could boast about at his own party congress. Accordingly, they revived some demands that they knew would be unacceptable, and left the Pan-European conference for the future. Yugoslav party sources have recently been quoted as estimating solemnly that at least six more months of work would be needed to prepare the conference.

Portugal: Cunhal vs. Democratic Eurocommunism

The effort to organize a European conference was not the only source of tension between the West European and Soviet Communist parties . . . [in 1975]. They also clashed in the so-called "Zarodov incident," the meaning of which is one of the great Kremlinological puzzles of recent years.

The incident took place against a background of recriminations and controversy in the Communist camp over the trend of events in Portugal. The controversy centered on the hard-line revolutionary tactics of Alvaro Cunhal, the Portuguese Communist leader. Both the Italian and Spanish parties viewed Cunhal's tactics as a disaster for the vision of communism to which they were committed. And in the course of attacking Cunhal, they created another of those situations that have done so much to blur the meaning of *communism*.

By the end of 1974, the Italian and Spanish parties were not only criticizing Cunhal but supporting his principal opposition in Portugal—the Socialist party of Mário Soares. In the fall of that year, the Italian and Spanish Communists conspicuously declined to send "fraternal delegates" to the Portuguese party's congress in Lisbon. Then, two months later, they *did* send delegates to the congress of the Portuguese Socialists. When the Socialists did far better than the Communists in the April 1975 elections to a constituent assembly, Spanish [Communist] party leader Santiago Carrillo expressed satisfaction with the results. They meant, he said, "that the Portuguese people, having put up with a half century of Fascist dictatorship, want nothing to do with dictatorships, of whatever type . . ."

. . . [In] summer [1975], when the Portuguese Communists were riding high and the Socialists were on the defensive, Soares appears to have made an effort to use his new friends in the Communist movement as leverage against Cunhal. First, he proposed an eight-party conference to discuss the situation in Portugal. The eight parties would be the Communists and Socialists of Portugal, Spain, Italy, and France. Soares got strong expressions of support from six of the eight and qualified support from the French Communists (who had been supporting Cunhal). But Cunhal himself just refused to have anything to do with the conference. Soares finally gave up on it.

Then he appears to have become intrigued by another possibility—the Italian Communists would intercede on his behalf in Moscow, and the Russians would then ask Cunhal to lay off. This idea actually had a certain logic to it: the desire of the Russians for the European party conference, and the central role of the Italian party in planning that conference, made it reasonable to suppose that the Italians would have a certain amount of bargaining power in any transaction with the Russians.

It is not entirely clear whether the idea of a mission to Moscow originated with Soares or with the Italians themselves. But it is known that in mid-July Gian Carlo Pajetta was in Lisbon talking to Soares. A few weeks later, he was on his way to Moscow. He arrived on August 6, having scheduled three days of talks with the Soviet leaders.

The Zarodov Episode

It appears that Pajetta got his answer from the Russians before he really had a chance to raise any questions. The issue of *Pravda* that appeared on the morning of August 6 featured a long article by a journalist and theoretician named Konstantin Zarodov. He is the editor of a journal that is published in both the Soviet Union and Eastern Europe; the Soviet edition is called *Problems of Peace and Socialism*. Zarodov had already used that journal to expound his hard-line Leninist views about the manner in which Communists should seize power. Now he was being given a chance to develop his ideas in *Pravda*. . . .

At first glance, the article did not look like anything that could stir up a great international controversy. . . . However, . . . the timing of publication to coincide with Pajetta's arrival, and a number of Zarodov's own formulations, suggest forcibly that he was writing with the ongoing row over Portugal in mind. . . . Perhaps the most arresting passages

. . . are those in which he criticizes "opportunist concepts" and "the present-day conciliators." The context makes it clear that these words refer mainly to the West European parties that have been acting like democrats. . . . "A revolutionary majority . . . is formed not only as a result of the creation of representative elective bodies of power but also in the course of direct revolutionary actions by the popular masses . . . going beyond the prosaic norms of a 'peaceful' life consistent with the bourgeois order."

Zarodov's parting shot at the conciliators is directed at their tendency to form alliances with other parties. He expresses horror at the willingness of some Communists to water down their revolutionary purity—to dissolve "the proletarian party . . . in an ideologically amorphous organization." . . . This is clearly a jab, not only at the Italian and Spanish parties but at the generally pro-Soviet French Communists, who have had a broad electoral alliance with the French Socialist party since 1972. [For strains in that coalition, see Jean-François Revel's article, "A Debate Between Two Lefts," in Section IV, below.—Ed.]

The USSR Line: Cunhal and Zarodov or the Popular Front?

In some respects the message conveyed by Zarodov seemed clear enough. It was certainly clear that the Russians were electing to stand pat with Cunhal. But . . . were the Russians seriously putting Cunhal forward as their model of how a Communist should operate these days? . . .

The initial reaction of the French party was to pass the article off as a mere historical essay. . . . Later, the paper . . . delivered a blistering attack on the article. The Italian party newspaper *l'Unità*, which also attacked it, suggested that it represented the views of only a hawkish minority in the Kremlin.

To students of Soviet affairs . . . the riddle of the Zarodov article centers on the fact that the author's advice to the West European Communists seems to be so bad. Any real effort by those parties to abandon their alliances and return to militant class warfare would surely lead to their isolation

and to heavy electoral defeats. . . . Many western analysts
have concluded that the Italian Communists were right
about the Zarodov article—that it represents only the views
of a hard-line minority in the Politburo. But . . . hardliners
in the Soviet leadership, . . . Boris Ponomarev [the Central
Committee's secretary in charge of relations with "nonruling" parties] and Mikhail Suslov, the Central Committee
secretary in charge of ideology, . . . were going on record
with some ideas quite different from his.

The Soviet magazine *Kommunist* . . . [in] summer [1975]
reprinted some speeches made by the two . . . [which] made
it clear that popular front tactics, which of course call for
Communists to form alliances with other parties, were again
appropriate today. . . .

The Soviet Message to Eurocommunists

Must we then conclude that the Zarodov article was just
an aberration—some peculiar misreading of the party line
by the editors of *Pravda*? This solution turns out to present
difficulties, too. A front-page news story in *Pravda* on September 18 [1975] reported solemnly that Brezhnev had just
met with Zarodov and expressed "high appreciation" of the
work being done by his magazine. . . . It is very hard to explain the meeting or its front-page treatment, except on the
assumption that Brezhnev was determined to put his own
prestige behind Zarodov's message.

Well, then, what *was* the message?

An answer that appears to make sense was proposed
recently by Leopold Labedz, the editor of *Survey*, a London-
based magazine specializing in Communist affairs. Labedz
suggests that the Zarodov article be read as a warning to the
Communist parties of Western Europe, and especially the
Italians. The essence of the warning is—don't go too far in
proclaiming your autonomy and your democratic principles;
don't create too many difficulties for us, about Portugal, or
Czechoslovakia, or Solzhenitsyn, or the conditions of the
European party conference.

And behind the warning is an implied threat. If the

leaders of the Italian party make too much trouble, the Russians just might order a major "turn" to the kind of Leninism that Zarodov was writing about. If the Russians ever did get behind any such international party line, they would, of course, be resisted fiercely by the leaders of the Italian and other Western Communist parties. But the Soviet leaders know that all those parties have many members for whom the Russian mystique is still very powerful, and for whom a real split with the Soviet Union would be intolerable. Thus any such split would be followed by splits in the ranks of those parties themselves.

The Threat to the Soviet Regime

From this interpretation of the Zarodov article, it would appear to follow that the Russians perceive the crisis of authority in the world movement to be intolerable. . . . For in all those arguments about what international communism stands for, much more is involved than the prestige of the Soviet leaders: what may ultimately be at stake is the legitimacy of their own regime and of the political system on which their own ruling class has erected its privileges.

If there are indeed "different roads to socialism," and if some of these permit a fair measure of political and cultural freedom, then why must the Soviet people be required to take the road of repression? On what basis can the Soviet leaders ask their own people to put up with the heavy-handed political controls they have endured for almost six decades? . . .

[In 1968] Brezhnev sent tanks into Prague because, he said, the Dubček regime was subverting the international cause by tolerating a measure of political democracy. Now Brezhnev and his colleagues are being asked to recognize as fraternal allies a sizable group of Communist parties whose heresies are far more extreme than Dubček's. In the view from the Kremlin, the crisis of authority in the international movement is a potential crisis for their own regime. Which suggests that the battle over the meaning of *communism* has not yet ended.

YUGOSLAVIA: NONTOTALITARIAN COMMUNISM [4]

Communism, Dalmatian Style

We all know that Yugoslav communism is different. Yugoslavia is not a captive member of the Soviet bloc and has adopted certain modifications of once orthodox practice, especially in economic matters. Nevertheless, Yugoslavia continues to define its social, economic, and political structures as "Marxist-Leninist" and "Communist." The Communist party holds a monopoly of political power. Its Tenth Congress was held while we were there, and the Soviet representative was all smiles as Tito boasted about the tens of thousands of members purged from the ranks since 1969 for opportunist or nationalist deviations from Marxism-Leninism. It is fair, then, to assume that what I was observing this spring was a variety of communism, even though it is not the only form that communism has taken or can take.

I shall here report some of the things I did in fact observe, selecting from those that might be presumed to throw some light on the quality of life under communism, Yugoslav style. . . . We covered only the Adriatic coastal area and the adjacent islands, and this region differs from the rest of Yugoslavia. Geographically it is separated by an almost unbroken line of high (and often splendid) mountains that cut off the coastland from the interior, so that, historically, this coastal-island region has been oriented westward across the Adriatic and specifically toward Italy. For many centuries the coast was Roman (most of it included in the province of Dalmatia), and for many centuries, somewhat later, it was ruled by Venice. Although ethnically the inhabitants became predominantly Slavic, with considerable Turkish admixture, as a result of the long series of invasions and conquests, a stronger flavor of Western and Mediterranean culture continues here and is spectacularly embodied in the still standing Roman, Byzantine, Medieval, Venetian, and Renaissance cathedrals, fortresses, walls, castles, churches,

[4] Excerpts from two articles by James Burnham, a staff editor. *National Review*. 26:755–7, 813–14. Jl. 5, 19, '74. Reprinted by permission.

houses, and entire walled cities. Still, however special Dalmatia may be, it is the red flag of communism, with its hammer and sickle, that now waves over Diocletian's palace and Dubrovnik's medieval Placa as over every village post office. . . .

Observations and Impressions

1. Yugoslavs are poor. Poverty is relative, so I must add: not poor compared to the inhabitants of Mali, Chad, or Afghanistan; very poor compared to people in West Germany, Belgium, France, or North America. But neither comparison is very illuminating. Using as standard roughly comparable non-Communist countries with which I have some direct acquaintance, it was my impression—confirmed by our Greek crew from a small village in Euboea—that their standard of living is below that of Greece, somewhat above Turkey's, more or less that of the poorer sections of southern Italy. Manufactured consumer goods were low in quality, high in price. Apart from some tourists and a few tourist facilities there were no signs of affluence or luxury; no fancy houses, no big cars, no expensive clothes, jewelry, or furniture, no luxurious shops, no big spending, no air conditioning outside of a few new tourist hotels. I saw lots of fat tourists, but almost no fat Yugoslavs.

2. There was nothing abject in this (relative) poverty. There were no beggars, no visible derelicts, no scrounging, no bowing and scraping. The children were well and cleanly dressed and obviously healthy. Most men wore the usual slacks and tieless shirt of the Mediterranean peoples. The clothing of the girls and women in the towns was inexpensive but rather tasteful.

3. Within the range of my observations, as I have indicated, this is an economically egalitarian society. I realize that Tito has his yacht, island retreat, and hunting lodge, and that as in all nations always and everywhere the ruling elite feathers its nests. But I can testify that not much feathering was done in any of the cities, towns, villages, and countryside that we covered. In a city of the non-Commu-

nist world the big gulf between rich and poor is obvious in a hundred ways: in the differences of neighborhood, dwellings, cars, furniture, restaurants, clothing, servants, pets. There are no comparable differences to be seen in Dalmatia. The most significant—and a not inconsiderable—difference was marked by possession of a car. Some Yugoslavs had cars, and most did not. All the cars were, however, sub-sub-compacts. But there just did not seem to be what could meaningfully be called "a wealthy class."

4. It was impossible to get accurate information about anything: everyone you asked contradicted everyone else. What stamps does it take to airmail a postcard to the United States? . . . [After many tries] finally we met a senior citizen who had spent his youth in San Diego. . . . He advised: "It doesn't matter what stamps you put on. Just mark it *par avion* and no one will notice the difference." Every problem connected with our boat got us into the same sort of maze. . . .

5. It was impossible to find out who was boss—a difficulty related to the contradictions. We could never be sure whether we were getting the word from the horse's mouth or from a junior pony's. . . . All over, in fact, there was an astonishing absence of brass of any kind, or, at any rate, of visible brass. There were scarcely any cops to be seen—none most places—and the few there were never did anything policelike. In the harbors, even the busy harbors of the larger towns, no one appeared to tell us where to tie up. We invariably had to figure it out for ourselves . . .

No one ever ordered us to do, or not to do, anything. In the country five kilometers outside Split are the partly excavated ruins of the ancient city of Salona, where Diocletian was born and Christians martyred. Most sites of such significance are, nowadays, fenced and guarded as closely as concentration camps. We went out by the regular city bus line—always one of the best ways to see a city and some of its residents. A few hundred meters from the bus stop, we found a wide open gate, with no guard or ticket collector, opening into the fields and hillsides where the ruins of basilicas and forums and ancient tenements lay here and there, with vines and potatoes and beans being cultivated beside and between them, and sheep and goats grazing where the martyrs had gone to the stake or the amphitheater. After we had been wandering about for an hour or so, . . . an apologetic caretaker appeared and asked us if we would mind paying a couple of dinar as entry fee. . . .

6. In towns of any size there were more or less standardized small supermarkets that I gathered were a state enterprise. But there were also open markets where the farmers (peasants) brought produce every morning. In the early hours the quality was generally good. . . . It was a delight to eat chickens that had scratched their food out of the ground instead of being force-fed in factories. Small shops, the many small woodworking, shoemaking, tailoring, and service operations, obviously belonged, like the markets and small fishing boats, to the private sector. The big hotels, the factories at Split, the big freighters and big ferry boats and shipyards I assumed to be government enterprises, like railroads, the telephone, the Jugobank, and the airline.

7. There was somewhat more marching or almost-marching than in other countries I know. In most towns in all countries you often see double lines of children being shepherded along by teachers or coaches, but I thought I saw them oftener than elsewhere. Several times there were lines of older students or maybe young Communists or soccer players marching and singing. The marching was not very solemn, however. The biggest parade we saw was in Kotor on the birthday of the Maximum Leader. . . . The parade went on for a half hour or so. . . . There were contingents of athletes and teams and clubs and schools, but everything was on a small scale with none of the strict discipline you see in the movies of Soviet, Chinese, or Nazi parades. . . . The squad leader put on quite a show of goosestepping, and the young soldiers had formidable submachineguns, but the watching girls and young men laughed and exchanged wisecracks. . . . A small group of officials . . . was in the reviewing stand, but when the parade was over they

mercifully disbanded without so much as a single speech.

8. In the larger towns, the European *Herald Tribune* (published by the New York *Times* and the Washington *Post*) and the leading newspapers and magazines of West Germany, France, and Great Britain were on sale to all comers and were bought and read without inhibition by both tourists and Yugoslavs. Bookstores carried books by foreign authors, in translation and in the original languages. Nearly all towns had at least one movie theater, and many of the films being shown were American.

9. There are many churches in the towns and villages along this coast, many of them of great architectural and archeological interest. Some have been made into museums and some are places of worship, and it is not always clear which is which. Circumambulating, one Sunday morning, the great twelfth century Dubrovnik walls, which measure up to 50 feet wide and 72 feet high, we could see the churches of the inner city. The bells of many were ringing. While we were passing next to the Dominican monastery a robed Dominican came out on a balcony, and we could hear a folk-music mass being sung. Many of the orthodox churches had the votive candles at hand, and lighted candles burning. In the little villages the churches seemed as integral as in little villages in most countries. But it was difficult to judge. The villagers and older people did not cross themselves or use a religious greeting or wear a little cross or medal as in many parts of Western Europe. In the shops there were crucifixes and icons, but not so many, and perhaps they were only art works or curios. It was my impression that religion was not dead, but not flourishing.

10. The Yugoslavs we met or dealt with in one capacity or another were not outgoing or spontaneously friendly, as Italians and Greeks can be; they had the roughness of most Mediterranean peoples; but they were civil. Though there were confusions and difficulties, none of us had any sort of "unpleasant incident."

11. Dalmatians are early-to-bed, early-to-risers. Nearly everyone seemed to be up and about by 6 A.M. Shops and

markets opened at 6:30 or 7:00 A.M., shut down at 11:00, and reopened from 4:30 to 6:30 or 7:00, the hours evidently set by regulation. Working hours for construction, mechanical jobs, offices, etc.. and even factories, were about the same. Everything, except a very few tourist places, shuts down at 10:00 P.M. In a restaurant—whether a dining room in one of the big new hotels or a small nontourist *gostione*—you would suddenly notice, if you kept at table close to 10:00 (which is not yet time to begin dining in many Mediterranean countries), that the waiters had changed into their street clothes. . . . In Dubrovnik there was a Casino "American style" (i.e., featuring craps and blackjack) . . . that was ready to stay awake as long as the players, but when we surfaced at midnight the streets were empty. In the smaller towns there were only two occasions when there was night life after 10:00: one on a Saturday night at Vela Luka, a little town at the head of a deep bay on the western end of Korčula island, when a rock combo played for a mixed tourist-Yugoslav crowd in a garden restaurant; the second, when our crew of five young Greeks, after we had all had a dinner together that included a good many glasses of Slivovitz, brought out their cassette player, and so cheerily showed the few post-ten strollers on the quay how Greek villagers dance that before long many of them were joining. . . .

12. No one appeared to be overworking. Few people did anything much in those long siesta hours. By 6:00 P.M. the *volta*—the evening promenade—was beginning along the main drag or quay, and everybody strolled for a couple of hours. The observable pace of construction workers, furniture makers, typists, was unstrained.

13. A final impression was not consciously formed until our first evening out of Yugoslavia. We had reached Bari [Italy] at twilight, and tied up in what turned out to be a huge, nearly empty, commercial harbor some distance from the city proper. But we located a pleasant small restaurant not far away, and after picking out some sprightly lobsters from the fish display, sat down at the only vacant table. And

the air around us was vibrating with the jabber and laugh-
ing and kissing and joking and coming and going of Italians
of all ages enjoying themselves over good food and drink
and each other. I realized that there had never been anything like this in Yugoslavia. The Yugoslavs did not look
gloomy, but they didn't ever seem to be having much plain
fun, the way you can so often feel as well as see and hear
Greeks and Italians having fun.

Communism or Communisms?

I ask myself: assume that I had known nothing whatever about Yugoslavia's regime, would I, on the sole basis
of the direct observations and impressions I reported . . .
[above], have been able to deduce that it was a Communist
country? Posters, signs, and occasional banners of the "Kommunist" (if I remember the spelling correctly) party, along
with the absence of any sign of any other party, could have
told me, but I will assume them, too, out of existence. I
could have known from the local papers, but my Serbo-
Croatian is restricted to the "good morning," "good evening," "where is the toilet?," "thank you," "how much?,"
"please" level. The frequent sight of the Maximum Leader's
picture would not have been a giveaway: that is characteristic of authoritarian governments of all sorts; Tito's picture
was not, for that matter, much more evident than Jack
Kennedy's used to be. I never saw a clenched fist or heard
a verse of the "Internationale."

I think the tipoff might have come, as the days went by,
from the failure to observe rich or even "well to do" Yugoslavs. I think I would have guessed that this probably had
something to do with communism. I am not raising the
question whether there actually *are* any rich Yugoslavs in
Dalmatia or elsewhere; I assume that some of the political
brass, managers, technocrats, and intellectuals, if not up to
Texan or West German standards, are well off in terms of
their de facto way of life, whatever their nominal incomes.
Nevertheless, in two weeks of covering a lot of ground, I did

not spot any rich Yugoslavs or any houses or cars or other stigmata that might have marked them.

This was, for me, a new experience. I have been in several dozen countries of diverse civilizations and races, and in every one of them I have observed—I could not have avoided observing—rich people. This is true of the poorest countries as of the richest (in fact, some of the richest people are to be seen in the poorest countries); of the most democratic countries as of the authoritarian; and it is true of countries with governments run by parties that call themselves "Socialist." Yugoslavian economic equality is certainly not of a Chinese strictness, but, comparing it with what I had previously known, I thought it something quite special.

No Fun Cities

The observation that Yugoslavs didn't seem to have much plain fun might also have suggested communism. The Communists and the Communist organizations I have known or known about haven't gone in for fun, and I gather there isn't much fun in Russia or Poland or Albania. But I am told that people do have fun in Budapest, Bucharest, and even Prague, so fun cannot be a principle of differentiation between communism and noncommunism.

Whether or not I would have recognized the scene as Communist without foreknowledge, knowing it suggested plausible explanations for some of the things we did observe. For example, the relaxed working pace could be explained as due to a lack of adequate incentive, for the average person at any rate, under the rules of a Communist economy. This could also explain the way the staffs of restaurants, stores, etc. signaled close-down hours; there isn't anything much, either at the moment or for the longer term, to be got out of keeping them open. The inaccuracy and vagueness of information as well as the difficulty in locating the person in charge could be interpreted as generalized buckpassing: if I don't say anything definite and don't take any responsibility, I won't get into trouble. Still, there are plenty of non-Communist countries where people don't work very strenuously; and the invisibility of bosses could, by itself, seem to point as much toward anarchy as toward communism.

I think that what I am getting at is that my own prior indirect knowledge and more recent direct observation confirm the prevailing (though not universal) view that, while the Yugoslav system can be meaningfully classified as "communism," it is not standard textbook communism; it is a variety of the species very different from Russian communism or Chinese communism.

The Totalitarian Test

I do not see how the Yugoslav regime can be called "totalitarian." As in totalitarian regimes, true enough, the government is an authoritarian dictatorship; there is a one-party political monopoly; there are severe restrictions on such political rights as free speech and on the rights of private property. But all these features, except perhaps the last, are typical of many sorts of dictatorship. The essence of the despotism, its pervasive extension to all or almost all of totalitarianism is the qualitative and quantitative breadth spheres of human action and interest: totalitarianism is the converged ultimate of the welfare state, the police state, and the ideological state. In our era the great exemplars are the Soviet, Nazi, and Chinese regimes, of which the Chinese is probably the closest approximation to the totalitarian ideal.

Like all contemporary states, Yugoslavia has totalitarian features, and more than most, but not enough to define the regime as totalitarian taken in its entirety. Hundreds of thousands of Yugoslavs work in Western Europe, going in and out. Millions of West European tourists, led by West Germans, are now visiting Yugoslavia every year. . . . Foreign journals and literature are available. The church is tolerated. Seven publicly dissident professors at the university are getting plenty of official criticism at the moment, but they are still talking and still have their jobs. We went where and when we chose. The state runs the key sectors of

the economy, but there are many outlets for private enterprise in small business, services, shops, food markets, and
crafts; and I am told there is more than talk in the Yugoslav
stress on worker-management (those waiters getting into
their street clothes at the appointed hour are possibly a
small instance). I mentioned . . . [above] the scarcity of police and the relaxed way in which people go about their
business or lack of business. On the Dalmatian coast most
people tune their TVs and radios to Italian stations. Things
of this sort just don't fit into a picture of totalitarianism.

Now as in the past, Yugoslavs get purged from the party
for political derelictions, sometimes lose their jobs, and
occasionally go to prison. I have heard from recent emi-
grants that even ordinary folk still get into trouble with
the authorities if they are stubborn about doing things their
own way. But the direct weight of the regime—and I think
this is true of many non-Communist dictatorships also—is
felt primarily by the political class and the intellectuals.
Since these are the talkers, the dictatorship can seem more
pervasive than it really is. Keep your nose out of politics
(and ideology) and it won't get punched may not always be
a safe rule, but it serves a prudent man as a fairly trust-
worthy guide most of the time. The net result is not model
democracy, but it is often less horrendous for the population
at large than the active opponents of the regime would have
us believe.

In modern times, western political and diplomatic doctrine has centered in the concept of the nation; the possibility of an ideological state is seldom taken seriously. Even
fully developed totalitarianism is thought of as in the last
analysis no more than an overlay on the basic, historically
controlling nation-substance. In keeping with this focus, we
distinguish from one another *Russian* Communism, *Chinese,
Polish, Yugoslav, Albanian* Communism, and build policy
on these distinctions. We pay less attention to the structural
and ideological differences among communisms, most notably the difference between totalitarian and nontotalitarian
communism, and seldom relate policy to this difference.

Totalitarian Détente

I have had and I retain not only a wholly negative view of totalitarian regimes but a cautious skepticism about the fruits of what is now called détente with such regimes, and about the net results to be expected from expanded trade and cultural relations. By the very nature of totalitarianism —a fact not hidden by totalitarian leaders—coexistence, détente, trade, and cultural exchange must operate to strengthen the totalitarian regime, and would not otherwise be undertaken. By virtue of being totalitarian, a regime is marked off as in opposition and hostility to the nontotalitarian world. By the nature of totalitarianism, therefore, détente coexistence, or whatever may be the wooing phrase of the moment can only be, from the perspective of the totalitarian leaders, as they have plainly affirmed, an alternate method of struggle, not a bid for friendship or cooperation. Moreover, détente, trade, cultural exchange, and tourism, under the totalitarian rules, do not serve to "open up" the totalitarian society; seem to serve more usually, as the Soviet dissidents have been trying to tell us, to deepen the repression.

Since the restrictions on policy toward the Soviet Union and China that this view of totalitarianism would impose have been breached at a dozen points in the Nixon-Kissinger pursuit of détente, it is rather nostalgic and abstract to bring the question up at what John Dean has taught us to call this point in time. Nevertheless, I want to stress, for the record if not for any practical purpose, my belief that the distinction between totalitarian and nontotalitarian communism is, or has become, meaningful, and relevant to the determination of policy. The factors that condemn the policy of détente to failure or, at best, sterility when attempted in relation to a totalitarian regime are sufficiently softened in the case of nontotalitarian regimes, even though Communist, to give a reasonable chance for mutual benefit from the expanded trade, cultural exchange, and tourism that political détente can encourage.

It is not merely the conflict between Yugoslav nationalism and Russian nationalism but the trend of the Yugo-slav regime away from integral totalitarianism that justifies the economic and cultural relations we have established with Yugoslavia during the years since Tito broke with Moscow. Given a still further expansion, Yugoslavian non-alignment might conceivably swing at least somewhat toward the Western side of the balance. (It is not a triviality that the international exchange value of the dinar is tied to the dollar, not the ruble.) With somewhat less assurance, similar reasoning would seem to apply to relations with Poland, Czechoslovakia, and Hungary, in whose regimes the totalitarian element, though more prominent than in Yugoslavia, is externally imposed and at least in some measure artificial.

True, there is a special risk in such a policy of active, enlarging relations with Communist countries, even if they are nontotalitarian. In Yugoslavia's governing and intellectual classes, as in the others', there are some—no one knows how many—Communist ideologues and some Soviet agents, for both of whom the interests of the world revolution and its Soviet fortress take priority in a crunch over national considerations. This means that there is always a chance that Yugoslavia may be pulled or pushed or driven all the way back into the orbit of Soviet totalitarianism; and Tito's death, which cannot be very far in the future, will be a critical moment for testing the odds. It would seem to me that . . . [a] policy of fawning on the Kremlin can only make that return seem, from a Yugoslav point of view, more sensible.

EASTERN EUROPE: CONSUMER UNREST AND CONCESSIONS [5]

The streets of Warsaw were overflowing with Christmas shoppers last week and they generally liked what they found. The stores were loaded with meat, and there were figs, dates and other treats of the season. Because if there

[5] From article "East Europeans Are Better Off," by David A. Andelman, foreign correspondent covering Eastern Europe. New York *Times*. sec IV, p 4. D. 25, '77. © 1977 by The New York Times Company. Reprinted by permission.

were nothing in the shops the other fifty-one weeks of the year, the week before Christmas would still be the week that counts for the increasingly powerful East European consumer, whose demands, many governments are beginning to realize, can make or even break a Communist regime.

Eastern Europe, much to the chagrin of and, indeed in contrast to, the Soviet Union, is starting to care more about its consumers. There is still, of course, a wide gap between East Germany, Poland and Hungary—countries prepared, at considerable cost and effort, to satisfy at least some of their consumers' aspirations—and others such as Rumania where consumers are being told that for a decade, perhaps more, their desires for a better life will still have to take a back seat to new factories and new steel mills.

Polish leaders have always stood or fallen largely on the question of how much was in the shops, particularly the meat shops. . . . [In 1970] when Edward Gierek replaced Wladislaw Gomulka as Communist party and government head, food riots were the catalyst. Now Mr. Gierek finds himself in much the same position as his predecessor, with severe meat shortages, a paralyzed economy and pressure for higher prices from the economists but consumers ill-prepared to pay them.

Mr. Gierek, as well as East Germany's Erich Hornecker and, to a lesser degree, most of the other leaders within the Soviet economic bloc, are gradually being forced to come to terms with what amounts to a revolution in rising expectations brought on by decades of increasing contact with the West and a channeling of political frustration into ambition for a more comfortable life. . . .

[In November 1977] East Germany, whose economy is generally acknowledged to be the most advanced in Eastern Europe, disclosed that it was spending the equivalent of $20 billion, a third of its national budget to subsidize consumer staples and services. . . . East German prices for bread, meat, milk, utilities, public transport and rent have not gone up in twenty years. But the subsidies have not prevented unfavorable comparisons between the quantity and particularly the quality of goods and services available in East Germany and that available in West Germany.

The difference between East Germany and Poland, where price subsidies are eating up close to a quarter of the national budget, is that in Poland during much of the year many goods are simply not available at any price. It still takes eight to ten years to obtain an apartment in Poland. Meat deliveries . . . [in 1977] were 5 percent lower than in 1976, and 1976 was down from 1975.

The dissatisfaction is compounded by the fact that Polish salaries have been rising steadily—over 40 percent . . . [between 1972 and 1977]. "Whenever the Polish worker gets a little more money in his pocket, he wants a lot more meat," said a Western diplomat. "What Gierek is going to have to do is take some of this excess purchasing power out of the Polish economy. But how he's going to do it, I still don't know."

The last time . . . [1976] that Mr. Gierek tried raising food prices—up to 60 percent in one stroke—riots broke out within hours of the announcement. Remembering the fate of his predecessor [Gomulka], he rescinded the increases within days. . . . [Since then] he has begun to look to a series of piecemeal solutions—a few more private shops, more imports of meat and grain—postponing the day of final reckoning.

Hungary: Goulash Communism

Hungary, by contrast, realized some time ago that the day of reckoning was at hand. Under a formula that came to be known as "goulash communism," the regime of Janos Kadar decided to satisfy consumer wants—raising prices, capitalist-style, at the same time—and slowing the rapid pace of industrialization. The result has been that while Hungarians, in terms of what their salaries can buy, pay double what Poles pay for meat, their complaints are much milder, involving such things as the lack of the latest-style clothes or long waiting lines for a new family car.

The Hungarian solution, which appears to be the one

that Poland, even East Germany and Czechoslovakia, may eventually choose, runs clearly counter to the Soviet model. But the Soviet Union has willingly, if not joyfully, offered its allies greater latitude in consumer matters in recent years, particularly since the Soviet leader. Leonid Brezhnev, was forced to concede the possibility of multiple roads toward socialism. The only Soviet requirement is that it all be done quietly.

Rumania and Bulgaria: Spartan Economies

Only two Soviet-bloc countries—Rumania and Bulgaria —have thoroughly retained the Soviet model in their handling of consumer affairs and their economies. Of the two, Rumania is clearly in the most difficulty. Bulgaria is no consumer's paradise, but by virtue of its decision more than twenty years ago largely at Soviet behest to concentrate on agriculture and mechanization, it is now able to feed its population well, even to export raw and finished agricultural products.

Rumania, by contrast, has developed neither an industrial establishment efficient enough to finance imports of food and consumer goods with industrial exports, nor an agricultural system adequate to satisfy domestic needs. Yet despite growing unrest from the coal miners of the Jiu valley to the factory workers of Bucharest and Brasov, the Rumanian president, Nicolae Ceausescu, told a Communist party conference . . . [in December 1977] that economic priorities would remain the same for eight more years.

The fundamental question being asked with urgency in Rumania, and with a growing degree of regularity throughout the Soviet bloc, is will the consumers wait. The answer cuts toward the heart of East Europe's disparate cultures and traditions to what one Western diplomat referred to . . . as "the threshold of pain." This threshold, comprised of food, clothing and the other necessities of life, relative social and political freedom plus an intangible admixture of history and temperament, varies from East European country to country. What would be bliss in Rumania, might cause riots in Warsaw.

One joke ever-popular . . . [in Poland] involves two dogs —one Polish, one Czechoslovak—who pass each other at the border. "Why are you going to Czechoslovakia?" the Czechoslovak dog asks the Polish.

"So that I can get something to eat," the Polish dog says. "But why are you going to Poland?"

"So that I can bark," the Czechoslovak dog replies.

II. THIRD-WORLD COUNTRIES: ASIA AND AFRICA

EDITOR'S INTRODUCTION

In countries under colonial domination—countries in which the exploiter is not a ruling class but a foreign power—nationalism gains new meaning, and national communism is often linked to wars of "national liberation." Although anticolonialism once unified what is now called the nonaligned movement, the Third World, as Walter Laqueur has observed (*Commentary*, February 1977), has little to unite it today. It includes countries belonging to OPEC (the Organization of Petroleum Exporting Countries) as well as the most impoverished nations; countries at war, like Ethiopia and Somalia; Communist and non-Communist countries; and dictatorships with Socialist names. However resistant they are to being colonies or satellites, newly independent countries have often sought the patronage of nations that are more technologically advanced, whether Communist or non-Communist. And competing factions within countries—Angola, for instance—have called upon the assistance of one superpower or another in their struggle for power.

The articles in this section present different facets of the pattern. The opening article, from the New York *Times Magazine*, describes the aftermath of the Vietnam war that dominated the 1960s. Next, Harold Isaacs, writing for the *New Republic*, analyzes Vietnam's long-standing hostility toward China, hostility that the United States ignored, he contends, in its effort to contain communism.

Two articles on Angola—one from *Nation*, the other from *National Review*—explore, from different perspectives, the tribal rivalries persisting in liberation movements and the way these exploit, and are exploited by, outside powers.

Last, a brief article on Somalia, from *Time* magazine, touches on the complex East-West relationships of Somalia and Ethiopia in the context of developing nationalism. Siad Barre, Somalia's president since 1969, has "nurtured nationalism, merging it with a blend of Marxism and Islam" (John Darnston, New York *Times*, March 19, 1978)—an endeavor in which he had Soviet assistance; part of that nationalism involved regaining the Ogaden region from Ethiopia. In July 1977, however, after Ethiopia severed its arms agreement with the United States, the USSR, hoping to win Ethiopia's allegiance, stepped in with assistance, thus arming both sides in the dispute after Somalia had occupied the area.

The *Time* article depicts Somalia at the point of its outraged break with the USSR and adoption of American patronage, prelude to several important developments: renewed warfare with Ethiopia, in which Somalia requested and was denied US arms aid; Ethiopia's recapture of Ogaden, with the help of USSR military advisers and Cuban troops, in February 1978; and President Carter's criticism of Soviet military involvement in the Horn of Africa in his March 17 address on US defense policy (excerpted in this volume in Section VI, below).

VIETNAM: AFTER THE FALL [1]

After the fall of the Thieu regime, Saigon is still a city in transition, half of it living in the past, the other half in a future partly undefined. The downtown bars are still mostly open, and in their empty dimness the bar girls still seem to be waiting for the return of their former patrons. The cafes, patterned on their Paris namesakes, are full. Lean youths in tapered shirts, long hair and flared jeans throng around the juke boxes, with their ceaseless blare of hard rock. Most of the French restaurants are still in business (though their French owners have left), and Saigon

---

[1] From article "Vietnamizing South Vietnam," by Max Austerlitz, a reporter on Asian affairs. New York *Times Magazine*. p 32-4+. Ap. 25, '76. © 1976 by The New York Times Company. Reprinted by permission.

still offers the best cheese soufflé and crêpes flambées in Asia.

The old bookshops have closed, but, thanks to the initiative of some enterprising merchants, literature for all tastes may be found spread neatly on the sidewalks—back copies of *Playboy* next to *U.S. News & World Report, The Gulag Archipelago* next to the *Encyclopaedia Britannica,* and a fair sampling of practically every book on Vietnam, in English or French, published over the past thirty years. The new bookshops that have been opened by the Provisional Revolutionary Government (PRG) display the writings of Ho Chi Minh, Marx, Engels and Lenin, as well as traditional Vietnamese literature and Saigon's new crop of newspapers. These include a paper published by the Saigon Revolutionary Committee; another published by an opposition figure under the old regime; a Chinese-language daily serving the Chinese ethnic community, and a Roman Catholic weekly.

The thieves' market is still thriving, with transistor radios, TV sets, stereo equipment, American records and other "preliberation" import items on sale at exorbitant prices. Cars and motorcycles have gone down in price, as a result of gasoline rationing; bicycles have gone up. At the central market, there is no shortage of goods or buyers. The whole city seems to be on a buying spree. Indeed, were it not for the absence of sandbags and barbed wire, and for the occasional portrait of Ho Chi Minh, it would appear to the casual observer that nothing had changed. The traffic is as chaotic as ever; an occasional child still begs on Tu Do Street; the English signs outside the bars and tailor shops remain untouched.

A Soft-Pedaled Revolution

This mélange of old and new is the result of deliberate choice. "All problems are important," explained one of the new leaders of South Vietnam, "but some are immediate and others can wait." The Vietnamese Communists made a distinction between "the essential and the nonessential" after coming to power in the South, and, since April 30, 1975, Saigon has been undergoing a step-by-step process in which the revolution has been soft-pedaled.

In the first few weeks after the entry of Communist forces, Saigon lived in a state that sometimes bordered on chaos. North Vietnamese soldiers set up billets; PRG cadres were in the process of identifying each other; Northern officials sent hastily from Hanoi were getting oriented, and the "304" was the scourge of the town. This—deriving from the numerals 30/4, for April 30—was the name the Saigonese had given to the "instant Communists" who emerged after the change of regime. They included a good number of petty crooks, whose favorite trick was to don black pajamas and go from house to house confiscating radios and TV sets in the name of "Socialist morality." For a while it was not easy for the population to tell the real cadres from the impostors. A few well-publicized executions of looters soon appeared to bring the problem under control. Another problem was the vast amount of guns, hand grenades and other weapons that flooded Saigon and other cities as the Saigon army disintegrated before the Communist advance. The authorities appear to have averted the potential danger to security by a collection drive in which weapons were turned in with no questions asked.

Next came the registration of all former government officials and military personnel, most of whom had returned to their homes in the cities. . . . Many of them hesitated to comply at first; those who did were given identity cards and advised not to change their domiciles. All but about 200,000 of the estimated 1.5 million persons affected were registered by June, and the "reeducation" process began.

For privates and most noncoms, this consisted of three days of lectures. For former officers, it entailed much more. Some 70,000 of them were sent to camps in the countryside, for a lengthy course of lectures and discussion meetings. In Saigon, the rumor was that the officers in the reeducation camps would have their eyes gouged out or

would be made to die of beriberi. . . . Rumors of bodily
harm in store for the officers have been squelched, but the
reeducation process has taken longer than had been generally expected. A few officers have returned, but the majority are still in the camps.

From Panic to Normalcy

In 1954, Saigon's population stood at 500,000. By 1974,
it had increased to more than 3 million, and the city had
become unmanageable. On April 30, 1975, the economy of
South Vietnam collapsed—and with it the legal system, the
public-order apparatus, the schools and the postal services.
All that was left was the cruel heritage of thirty years of
war.

To govern the country, the Communists set up Military
Management Committees in all the provinces, and a separate one for the Saigon area. In the provinces, control was
turned over to civilians after a few months; Saigon, however, was a festering sore. Its swollen refugee population;
the long years of unnatural dependence on imported raw
materials; the warped market economy in which hoarding
and the creation of artificial shortages by some businessmen
had been the rule; the tens of thousands of orphans,
cripples and prostitutes—all this made for a situation that
was to tax the new authorities to the utmost. The Saigon
Military Management Committee—actually, 7 of its 11 members were civilians—remained in place as a precaution
against potential disturbances and as a handle for the
superlative administrative system of the North Vietnamese
army.

The intervention of the NVA in the city government
seems to have been dictated by necessity. The southern-
based PRG was well entrenched in the countryside, but it
had only a skeleton organization in Saigon and no experience in managing large urban centers. Cadres had to be
rushed in from the North. Some of them were southerners,
former Vietminh members who had moved North after the

1954 Geneva Agreements and who now rediscovered a Saigon they hardly recognized.

I arrived in Saigon two days after liberation [said one of them], and the first thing I did was to go and visit members of my family whom I had not seen for twenty years. I found them all, eighteen of them, in the house of an uncle of mine, clustered in one room and shaking with fright. I asked them what was wrong. "We know the Communists are going to kill us," they said, "so we all came here so we would die together." I told them to stop being foolish and to go back to their homes.

For 10 days [the official added], they were in a state of bliss. Today, all they do is complain. Not enough gas, the shops are running out of soda water, they no longer get the latest French fashion magazines.

The Saigon city government is now staffed by a mixture of PRG cadres, southern "returnees" from the North, northerners of the Hanoi mold, and a sprinkling of former Saigon technical personnel trained in American methods. The combination has worked surprisingly well. At the Saigon airport, for instance, the former ground personnel and meteorological staff are back at work under the direction of North Vietnamese supervisors, and the lumbering C-130s, on which the Saigon emblem has been replaced by the North Vietnamese star, are given their landing instructions by the same American-trained air-traffic controllers who operated the control tower during the days of President Thieu.

Saigon: Administering Reconstruction

A good way to understand how the Saigon city government goes about its task is by studying the organization of one of the eleven districts into which the greater Saigon area has been divided. The Son My Tay district lies in the outskirts of Saigon. It has a score of industrial plants, including four cotton mills, a sugar refinery, a producer of native drugs and an ice-making factory, and some small—mostly family-run—food stores, carpenter shops, repair shops and the like. There were at most 100,000 inhabitants in Son My Tay in 1965; by the late sixties the number reached 200,000.

Son My Tay is administered by its own Revolutionary
Committee, under the guidance of the overall city management group. The committee oversees the work of nine departments, in such areas as the economy, education, information and culture, public security, health and welfare and
other concerns. Apart from that, the district is divided into
subdistricts of 10,000 to 20,000 people, which are subdivided into sectors of up to 5,000 people, which are further
subdivided into "solidarity units" of about twenty families
apiece. Overlapping these subdivisions are any number of
associations of teachers, intellectuals, shopkeepers, young
people, women, workers, religious groups and so on. Within
this system, the individual becomes part of a web of mutual
responsibilities. For instance, at the simplest level, sanita-
tion in Saigon's back streets is now the responsibility of the
"solidarity units," operating through the local workers',
young people's and women's associations.

The chief problems in Son My Tay were economic. The
unemployment rate in the months after "liberation" reached
70 percent—a reflection of a situation on the national level
in which more than three million people, including about
one million military, became jobless overnight a year ago.
Economic recovery in Son My Tay has been facilitated by
the absence of large industries dependent on imported raw
materials. Except for one plant, all the industries in the
district were privately owned under the former regime, and
still are. "Our policy," said Nguyen Chi Hieu, chairman
of the Son My Tay Revolutionary Committee, "consists,
first, of normalizing life within our district, and, second,
of assisting those who were displaced by the war and had
to move to the city to return to their homes in the countryside."

"Return to the Countryside": A Central Strategy

"Return to the countryside"—everything in the new
leaders' plans hinges on that. Between 1965 and 1975, approximately 10 million South Vietnamese—more than half
the population of the country—were displaced from their

village homes. The rural population decreased from 85 percent of the total to 47 percent. While some of the villagers moved from one rural area to another, the major displacement was from the countryside to the cities. More than five million of the refugees are today crowded in the cities —Saigon, Danang, Nha Trang, Hue, My Tho, Vung Tau —where they are partly or totally out of work. The new government is faced with the problem of not having enough farmers to till the land, and too many urban residents who are out of work or who have skills of little use to the economy.

Rural resettlement, an operation of staggering proportions, is being implemented along two lines. One is called "return to the village of origin." This will affect those displaced persons who have maintained roots—family, some property—in their birthplaces. While the government is providing some help, this program does not require a major effort, as people will be returning to areas where they already have some economic foundation.

However, in many cases the original village has been totally destroyed, together with the ancestral tombs, and the land has lain untended, with the result that the displaced persons have lost their attachment to the place. In other cases, the village does not have enough arable land to support the returnees with their enlarged families. So a twin program is the establishment of rural "areas of new economy," where displaced persons who don't want to go back to their old villages can be resettled and rehabilitated, and where new opportunities can be offered for young volunteers. . . .

In Vietnam, a village usually consists of a cluster of hamlets covering an area of up to 25,000 acres and housing about 1,000 families, or 5,000 to 8,000 inhabitants. About five hundred villages are to be rebuilt. A displaced person is given a choice of returning to his village, whether inside or outside an area of new economy, or moving to a new location inside such an area.

A lot must be done before such a zone is ready to re-

ceive the refugees. First, the mines and unexploded ord-
nance must be disposed of and the bomb craters must be
filled. Then, a start must be made on reclaiming the land,
restoring the wells, laying new roads and building the
houses, medical centers, and other facilities. Only then will
the displaced persons begin to arrive—and to assist in the
subsequent work of reconstruction.

Each family that moves in receives a basic kit of farming and cooking utensils, mosquito netting and other rural
necessities, as well as enough food to last it until the first
harvest. Each family is also given 10,000 square meters
(about 2.5 acres) of land. The family will have deeds to the
land, but any part of the crop it wishes to sell must be sold
to the state at fixed prices. In addition, however, each family will be given a "private plot" of 300 square meters
(about 3,230 square feet), the produce of which it will be allowed to sell at free prices on the free market.

The program, which began to be implemented at the
end of 1975, calls for resettling and rehabilitating five million people over the next three to five years. Of these, it is
expected that three million will move to areas of new
economy and two million will return to their villages outside those zones. . . .

The question could naturally arise as to whether there is
an element of coercion in the resettlement policy. The answer could perhaps be best stated as follows:

All available statistics indicate that the great bulk of
the displaced persons who moved to the cities during the
war were farmers. It is obvious to anybody who has spent
any time in South Vietnam that the great majority of these
refugees, who have been living in urban slums, are eager to
go back to their accustomed environment—the countryside
—and resume their lives as farmers. Indeed, all the evidence
on the spot indicates that so far, at least, more people have
applied to go back to the countryside than the new regime
has been able to process. It would, therefore, appear unlikely that, at least at this stage, the government would
want to coerce people into moving to the countryside while

there are long lists of volunteers waiting to go. . . .

Certainly, from its gradualistic approach and the form it seems to have taken thus far, the South Vietnamese re-settlement program is markedly different from the more radical process that is reported to have taken place in Cambodia—as the origins, nature and history of the Vietnamese revolution have been markedly different from those of the Khmer Rouge [native Cambodian Communists].

Another question that could legitimately arise is whether, after all the years of bitter fighting, there is any retribution under way against the defeated side. All that can be said with any degree of certainty by a Western observer who has spent a comparatively limited span of time in the country is that there is no sign of any major retribution and no rumors to that effect. At the same time, it is obviously impossible for any outside observer to see the whole country. . . .

Unification

Vietnamese, North and South, . . . [in 1975 elected] a national assembly for all of Vietnam. It . . . [was] the first formal step toward reunification of the two parts of a country . . . divided by the 1954 Geneva Agreements into what were to have been two "temporary zones" pending national elections in 1956. From the standpoint of the Vietnamese Communists, they are now implementing a process they feel was aborted twenty years ago. As Mr. Hieu, of the Son My Tay Revolutionary Committee, put it,

You must understand that for us, since 1945, the Vietnamese revolution was one. We are all Vietnamese and we all fought for the same ideal. So what does it matter if one of us was born in one Vietnamese province rather than in another?

All the provinces of the country, from the Camau Peninsula in the extreme south to Lang Son in the far north, have been redesigned, bringing the combined total down from 62 to 34. The two provinces on either side of the 17th parallel have been joined, symbolically, into one. . . . The succeeding phases of social and economic unification will proceed, step by step, for an unspecified length of time. The reasons are pragmatic.

Throughout the war years, inflation was endemic in the South, and currency was printed with little regard to the economic situation. . . . By May 1975, the currency's backing had dissolved to nothing. To prevent the South's inflation from being exported to the North, the two halves of the country had to be sealed from each other, in terms of financial transactions.

In September [1975], the Provisional Revolutionary Government announced that the Saigon piaster would be replaced by a new currency. Everyone would be permitted to exchange up to 10,000 old piasters into new piasters at a rate of 500 to 1; any old piasters in excess of that amount would be blocked in a special bank account until their origin could be established. Not surprisingly, news of the impending reform leaked, and wealthy Saigonese started devising ways of circumventing the operation.

One of the most original was to register at the French-run Hôpital Grall. Patients in the first-class wards were required to make an advance deposit for a fifteen-day stay; on checking out, the unused portion was refunded. On the day before the currency exchange, a good number of well-to-do Saigonese suddenly fell sick and were admitted to the hospital. Once the exchange was in train, they were all miraculously healed and claimed the unused part of their deposit in the new currency. By the third day of the exchange, the first counterfeit bills appeared.

Easing the Transition

On the whole, however, the currency exchange went off fairly smoothly, and the officials chose to turn a blind eye to the relatively few instances of petty cheating, which occurred mainly in Saigon, . . . [to] avoid . . . exacerbating fears or suspicions, so that the transition . . . [could] proceed with a minimum amount of friction. . . .

While most of Saigon's streets have been renamed, the new street signs give the old names in smaller characters under the new ones, so as to avoid confusion. On a more important level, the new officials seem to recognize that the farmers who go back to their villages are not the same simple country folk who came to the cities years ago.

Many of the displaced persons [said a high-ranking official in Hanoi] picked up new habits. Some of the habits were bad and contrary to our traditions. Others were socially less significant. They got used to electricity, refrigerators, soft drinks and the like. On this, there is no going back, and we will realize that there are now new requirements to be satisfied.

Cultural Restoration

This touches on what appears to be a rather sensitive issue in Vietnam these days. During the war, the North suffered considerably more than the South in terms of material destruction, but it emerged with its social structure intact and its wealth—whatever there is of it—divided equitably. In the South, there are many more consumer goods than in the North, but they are unevenly distributed and their cost in terms of social disruption has been tremendous. It is therefore hardly surprising that many of the revolutionary cadres who have returned to Saigon after an absence of more than twenty years have been profoundly disturbed by what they perceive as the cultural prostitution of their native city.

It would be a mistake to regard this reaction as essentially xenophobic. Many of these cadres are French-educated, and schooled in the subtleties of French literature. Yet, while they have had no difficulty in assimilating French culture to their Vietnamese upbringing, the superficial but glaring Western influence that has pervaded many of the everyday aspects of life in Saigon leaves them repelled. This feeling is echoed in the Communist press, which constantly refers to the former regime's alleged uninterest in the fostering of Vietnamese literature, art and traditions.

Thus, if there is a term that can be used to describe what South Vietnam is undergoing, it is Vietnamization. Apart from any political or ideological considerations, Vietnam is reclaiming its soul. Whether in the field of literature or music, or even the manufacture of goods for everyday use, Vietnam is now looking inward to its own resources. Fifteen years ago, mats were made from reeds. These were then replaced by imported plastic strips. Today, mats in South Vietnam are again being made from reeds.

Economic and Social Integration:
State vs. Market Economies

On the national level, North and South face a series of fundamental choices. The North has a state of cooperative economy; the South, for all practical purposes, has a market economy; how will the two economies be fused? The North has one of the best educational systems in Asia; the schools in the South have just reopened; how will the young people of the two zones be raised to a common outlook? The North has an extensive health service; the South is facing a shortage of medical drugs, and is hampered by the urban focus of its medical facilities; how will a reunified nation aspire to uniformity in health care? In the North, the major energy source is coal, of which there is an ample supply. In the South, the major source is oil, which has to be imported. While there is a good chance that oil might be found in the South, will the Vietnam of tomorrow be dependent on coal, on oil or on both? On that question alone, the choices to be made will necessarily entail the involvement of foreign expertise.

Refugees and Would-Be Refugees

On June 27, 1975, the first foreign aircraft landed in the reopened Saigon airport. It was a plane of the United Nations High Commissioner for Refugees (UNHCR), inaugurating the first airlift of food and medical supplies to Saigon under the new regime.

The emergency operation, launched in March 1975 under the aegis of Secretary General Kurt Waldheim, had been . . . [disrupted by] the fall of Saigon. . . . By the time the operation tapered off in August, it had delivered some 19,000 tons. . . .

The reopening of the air link to the outside world was greeted with relief by the several thousand foreigners who had been left stranded in Saigon. The great majority of Americans had left the city before the entry of the Communist forces, but the French had stayed on. They included diplomats, businessmen and longtime residents of Vietnam, as well as several hundred teachers and technicians who were there under the auspices of the French aid program. While there were no reports of any harassment of Westerners, the foreigners by June were out of work or out of money or both. The Saigon Military Management Committee set up a special department to expedite exit visas for foreigners, and some five hundred of them, including a number of Americans, were flown out by the UN. With the end of the UN airlift, the French government took over and chartered an aircraft, which now flies the Saigon-Bangkok route five times a week, principally for the purpose of bringing out foreigners.

Both UNHCR and the United Nations Children's Fund have had programs in Vietnam since early 1974, covering the former Saigon regime's areas, the PRG areas and the North, and both agencies now have offices in Hanoi and programs throughout the country. UNHCR has also made its good offices available for other humanitarian purposes. Thus, it repatriated nine Americans who had been captured in the South, and were released in Hanoi, and it flew out the bodies of three American pilots who had been listed as missing in action. The bodies were transported on the same UNHCR aircraft that brought to Hanoi a congressional delegation headed by Representative G. V. Montgomery, Democrat of Mississippi, last December [1975].

Foreign Aid and Enterprise

Apart from UN assistance, which now includes programs of the World Health Organization and the Food and Agriculture Organization, Vietnam is receiving a much greater amount of help from individual countries on a bilateral basis. The Soviet Union and China are still the major donors, but help is also coming from smaller nations. The Cubans have built a hotel in Hanoi and have repaired several roads. Sweden is building a paper mill. Some aid is also being given by private organizations such as the International Committee of the Red Cross, and by American religious groups such as the Quakers and Mennonites.

Indeed, the end of the war has reopened Vietnam to the outside world. The Japanese company that built the Danhim Dam in South Vietnam was recently requested to continue its work. A French oceanographic vessel is mapping the seabed off South Vietnam, and Vietnamese students have been sent to countries like Australia and Switzerland. And the country's Communist leaders have indicated that they envisage eventual joint ventures with Western companies to develop the country's resources.

The overriding preoccupation today, however, is with tasks of reconstruction that can only be accomplished by the Vietnamese themselves. "We won the war," said a high-ranking official in Hanoi, "and we will now prove to the world that we can win the peace."

What could well emerge from this effort is a new Vietnam of 45 million inhabitants with qualities acknowledged by both friend and foe, with considerable natural resources, with the best army in Southeast Asia, and with a profound sense of its national and cultural identity. Such a nation would be certain to play an increasing role in the world.

VIETNAM: NATIONALISM, CHINA, AND AMERICAN POLICY [2]

Indochina was the scene but China was the backdrop of the drama . . . , the stage strewn with corpses and filled with dazed and uncomprehending survivors. Vietnam and Cambodia is where the action took place, but for reasons why it all happened one has to look beyond to China. These reasons do not make "sense" out of what Americans did in

[2] From an article entitled "Our SOBs," by Harold R. Isaacs, former foreign correspondent, author, professor of political science at MIT. New Republic. 172:4–5. My. 3, '75. Reprinted by permission.

Indochina but they do come closer to "explaining" what the Americans thought they were doing there.

The China background is there from beginning to end of the whole long bloody story. The ultimate irony is that all the protagonists in the Vietnam tragedy shared feelings and perceptions relating to China that were at bottom more alike than different, enough to have produced quite different outcomes. It is at least possible to imagine such outcomes well within the political realities as they existed after the middle of 1945. But the actors in this drama saw their differences as greater than their alikenesses and therefore slew each other in great numbers for year after year. . . .

Vietnamese Nationalism

Vietnamese nationalism, Communist or non-Communist, was directed against France. But France ruled Indochina for less than a century. Long before France, China was the prime foe of Vietnamese independence, in imperial times a demanding suzerain, in more recent times a claimant to controlling influence. When Ho Chi Minh and his Communist nationalists proclaimed independence in Hanoi in 1945, . . . [the Vietnamese] had a Kuomintang Chinese occupation force to deal with and they saw China as the power with which they would have to deal, beyond France, if they were to stay free of foreign rule or control. This became more, not less, of a fact after Communist China replaced Kuomintang China on their northern frontier. In those years Ho Chi Minh showed a readiness to be flexible in any direction that would move him toward his nationalist goals. Ho was a Communist, but as he plainly indicated himself in 1945, and as his whole career and indeed the course followed by his successors showed, Vietnamese communism was as nation-centered as Stalin's, Tito's and Mao's, perhaps even more so. It is impossible to say what might have happened had the United States in 1945 had the capacity and the wit to play the game into which Ho invited it. The results could hardly have been more disastrous than those that came out of the course the United States followed instead.

US Policy

It began in 1945 by acquiescing in and then actively aiding the return of the French to their former colony at the end of the war with Japan. The reasons for this were many: ignorance and indifference, Europe-centered myopia, a view of the world that assigned greater weight to recovery of French power than to the unwillingness of Vietnamese to remain under French rule, an inability to see that the renovation of all politics and all power systems in Asia after the defeat of Japan would not wait on American conceptions of timetables and priorities, or conform on naive demand to American images of the world and its peoples.

When power in China passed to the Communists, all these elements, and more, fused into an American policy that desperately and more and more blindly tried to throw up bulwarks against what was seen as an onrushing Communist tide. The reality of the new Chinese reality was somber enough; in American minds it was feverishly enlarged by all the swiftly reappearing images of threatening vastness and numbers, swarming hordes, inscrutability, devilish cleverness, the yellow and red perils rolled into one great fearful lurid menace to American power and security, indeed to human well-being and survival. . . .

Despite alarm, pressure and great debate, war weariness had made it impossible for the United States to intervene with force in 1948–1949 on behalf of Chiang Kai-shek's regime as it fell apart, partly under Communist onslaught, mostly from its own inner rot. This plunged America into the hysterical spasm of McCarthyism and the hunt for those who had "lost" China. But what the United States did do, as that spasm was at its height, was to go to the aid of the French and their puppet emperor Bao Dai in what had become a war for the control of Indochina.

When the French and their Vietnamese clients—Nguyen Van Thieu was an officer in their army—were defeated by the Communists at Dien Bien Phu in 1954, President Eisenhower managed to resist John Foster Dulles' appeal to him to rescue them by sending in American airpower. But in

short course the Americans picked up where the French had
been forced to leave off. It was as though no one remembered how a million Japanese had bogged down in China,
and how the more recent American experience of stalemated
war in Korea had led some of America's best military com-
manders—McArthur and Ridgeway—to warn the country
never again to engage its forces on the Asian mainland. It
was as though the experience with Chiang had taught us
nothing about tying our fate to leaderships incapable of
maintaining a viable base of support among their own
people. In a short few years, the French war in Indochina
became America's war, a war to hold a "line" in Southeast
Asia against Communist China. Having avoided disaster in
China, and barely escaped it in Korea, the United States
plunged on resolutely to meet it this time in the morass of
Vietnam.

It was a mordantly neat touch of historic punctuation
therefore, that death should come to Chiang Kai-shek,
whose American-trained and equipped armies collapsed so
ignominiously in China, during the very week that Nguyen
Van Thieu's American-trained and equipped armies were
collapsing, twenty-six years later and even more ignominiously, in Vietnam, yielding province after province in a
pellmell flight that opened the way to a Communist takeover. It was a "coincidence" that would have been absurd
dramatic license in art; it could only happen in nature.

US-Chinese Détente

Chiang Kai-shek lived out most of the years of his exile
on Taiwan clinging to the hope that the Americans who
"failed" him in 1949 would finally go to war against Communist China and enable him to realize the dream of the
return that sustained him. Instead, in 1971, the United
States resumed relations with Communist China. The American President who had launched his political career by
mercilessly pillorying those Americans who he said had
"lost" Chiang Kai-shek's China ended up by "finding" Mao
Tse-tung's.

This new twist in the turn of the power struggle abruptly made the "reason" for all the blood and sacrifice in Indochina inoperative. It had to be shredded or at least filed away until some new twist and new turn in the future required it to reappear. What had to be done now was to extricate the American forces from the Vietnamese morass into which they had sunk. This was accomplished with matchless cynicism and virtuoso skill by the Kissinger "peace agreement" that allowed the Americans to leave and the war to go on, for a "decent interval," to its foregone conclusion.

It was foregone because the Thieu leadership in Vietnam —and Lon Nol's in Cambodia—like Chiang's in China, was simply incapable of providing a viable political leadership with strong enough roots in the country and its people to maintain itself. The most disastrous of all the illusions that took us into this course of action was the belief that American power could fill the vacuum created by the weakness and failures of the leaders, classes, political parties and movements whom we found ready and willing to profit by allying themselves with our cause.

Unlike plays in the theater which do end, this one will go on and on. Beyond the bloody scenes yet to come, beyond the next intermission—some new "decent interval"—it is not too difficult to guess the opening scene of a new cycle to come: it will show some mini-Kissinger arriving secretly at a secret rendezvous—in Peking, perhaps, or Hanoi itself —to open negotiations with some mini-successor to [Vietnam's] Ho Chi Minh.

ANGOLA: FROM TRIBE TO NATION [3]

For the ten months preceding independence on November 11, 1975, I was a graduate student living in Luanda and observed at first hand during that turbulent period the na-

[3] From an article, entitled "Report from Luanda: A New Angolan Society," by Kevin Brown, Fulbright Fellow in Portugal and Angola 1974-1975, researching the development of nationalism in Angola. Nation. 223:42-6. Jl. 17, '76. Reprinted by permission of The Nation Associates, 333 Sixth Av., New York, N.Y. 10014.

tion-building activities of the MPLA [Popular Movement for the Liberation of Angola], the liberation movement whose ideology and program will profoundly affect the future of Angola. I am convinced that the foundations of a new Angolan society have already been established and that, despite the experimental nature of much that has been accomplished, the general outlines of the radical transformation now in progress can be observed.

Three Liberation Movements: Rival Tribes

The debate in this country over the government's involvement in Angola tended to obscure rather than clarify the complexities of the Angolan civil war. When Secretary of State Kissinger attempted to justify covert aid to the FNLA [National Front for the Liberation of Angola] and UNITA [National Union for the Total Independence of Angola] by characterizing them as "pro-Western" and "anti-Communist" he erroneously injected an ideological element where none really existed. The Angolan civil war was not a miniature East-West confrontation but an internal power struggle between rival tribal groups whose interest in ideology is comparatively recent. The Mbundu and Bakongo peoples, bitter rivals today under the banners of their respective liberation movements, the MPLA and the FNLA, have been fighting each other intermittently since the beginning of the slave trade in Angola. The animosity is so deep that even a fourteen-year guerrilla war against their common enemy, the Portuguese colonial regime, failed to bridge their ethno-linguistic differences. Indeed, it is only a slight exaggeration to argue that the Angolan civil war actually began in 1961 with the outbreak of the liberation struggle, inasmuch as the MPLA and the FNLA (and after 1966, UNITA) often fought each other more than they did the Portuguese. [For further information on UNITA see the article that follows.]

It is true that the three movements attempted to exploit the East-West rivalry to garner military aid, and it is also true that the MPLA triumphed after receiving massive

amounts of such aid from the USSR and Cuba. Yet the
MPLA's victory is by no means a victory for communism
nor would the United States necessarily have gained concessions if the FNLA/UNITA coalition had won. The Angolan movements are above all nationalistic and dedicated
to the elimination of all forms of foreign domination. As
far as the MPLA is concerned, its ideology is best described
as African socialism, with the emphasis on "African" to the
extent that it represents an adaptation of classical European
Marxism to the African situation. While the MPLA accepts
the Marxist view of the world as divided between the capitalist exploiters and the proletarian exploited, it substitutes
for the concepts of the class struggle and private property the
concept of African autonomy: political, economic and cultural. The colonial experience taught the MPLA leadership
that the crucial issue is not whether the means of production are owned publicly or privately but that they be controlled by Africans who are free of colonial and neo-colonial
attitudes.

Thus the program the MPLA intends to implement
sounds much like the typical platform of a European social
democratic party. It calls for a republican, secular and democratic regime with independent legislative and executive
branches; state control of basic industries and energy resources, with provision for private commercial activity, foreign or domestic, as long as African interests are served;
education and social welfare facilities for all Angolans. In
short, there is nothing obviously "communistic" about the
MPLA's program. Whether or not the new Angolan society
eventually turns Communist is another matter, but there
is no ideological predisposition for such an outcome.

It is one of the ironies of Angolan history that the April
1974 coup in Portugal which signaled the demise of the
Portuguese colonial empire, came at a time when the liberation struggle was at the nadir of its effectiveness. The three
movements, fighting among themselves and consequently
incapable of more than mild harassment of the Portuguese
army, appeared to be further than ever from their objective

of an independent Angola. For the MPLA, the situation was particularly grave; an internal factional dispute, compounded by the Soviet Union's decision to suspend aid because of disenchantment with the MPLA's poor showing against the Portuguese, threatened its very survival. The dispute involved charges by the leaders of two factions that President Agostinho Neto had subverted the democratic principles of the MPLA by refusing to delegate authority and acting in a dictatorial manner.

Daniel Chipenda, an Ovimbundu and leader of the "Revolt of the West" faction, eventually defected to the FNLA, along with several hundred of the MPLA's best guerrillas; the "Active Revolt," led by the Andrade brothers, chose to dissociate themselves from Neto while nominally remaining within the movement. The latter faction is composed mostly of *mestiço* [mestizo, of mixed parentage] intellectuals who had played a prominent role in the MPLA since its inception in 1956. Although Neto survived this challenge to his control and emerged as the recognized leader who would represent the MPLA in decolonization negotiations with the Portuguese, the rift with the Active Revolt continues to be a source of tension and could be a factor in future power struggles within the MPLA.

If Neto's organization entered the period of transition to independence somewhat shakily, it nevertheless had certain advantages over the other movements. First, the MPLA's long-standing ties with the Portuguese Left secured it preferential treatment from army and government officials, many of whom openly sided with the MPLA against its rivals. Second, it had the advantage of fighting in its own tribal area during the battle for control of Luanda. Third, and most important, the Soviet Union and Cuba were willing to provide almost unlimited support in advisers and materiel, in sharp contrast to the United States aid to FNLA/UNITA which never matched what the MPLA received either in quality or quantity. MPLA's edge in military hardware ultimately proved decisive in winning the civil war, but at the inauguration of the transition government in January 1975, victory was by no means a foregone conclusion. Soviet arms (Cuban "advisers" arrived in force in June) did no more than permit the MPLA to hold its own against the FNLA in the battle for Luanda.

The Debacle of Transition: Bureaucratic Infighting

The transition government, designed to facilitate an orderly transfer of power to the three movements, was a disaster from the start. Everybody shares the blame for the debacle: the Portuguese, for having done little to prepare the colony for independence; and the three movements for having failed to end their internecine quarrel during the fifteen years of the liberation struggle. About the only positive thing to be said of the transition government is that it is unique in the annals of African decolonization. Nothing so complex had heretofore been created. The four interested parties divided up twelve ministries more or less evenly, the more sensitive ones such as Interior (police) and Information being equipped with watchdog secretaries from the rival movements. At the top, the movements rotated the premiership monthly, while the Portuguese High Commissioner sought to insure the observance of the provisions of the Alvor Accords, which were the legal basis for the government. This cumbersome, unwieldy structure guaranteed that bureaucratic infighting would replace effective administration, an unpromising situation that proved fatal because of the presence in Luanda of four mutually hostile armies, each itching for an opportunity to settle old scores. [For further information on the Alvor agreement see the next article in this section.]

The explosion came in late March [1975] and for the next four months Luandans lived in a nightmare. As many as ten thousand Africans may have died in the crossfire of machine guns, mortars and rocket-propelled grenades that caught them defenseless in their fragile tin-roofed huts. Between outbreaks of heavy fighting that flared up with depressing regularity, first in the African *musseques* or shantytowns and later in the white neighborhoods, Luandans were subjected to individual acts of terrorism. Known supporters of the movements daily ran the risk of robbery, rape, kidnap and assassination. A *mestiço* friend of mine, himself the victim of an FNLA kidnapping, described the atmosphere in the *musseques* as a "human rabbit hunt."

Repeated attempts to resolve this state of unofficial civil war foundered upon the conflicting strategic interests of the two main antagonists: the MPLA and FNLA. For the FNLA, a firm foothold in Luanda was essential if it hoped eventually to control Angola. However, the lack of tribal support there, where the Bakongos accounted for only 10 percent of the population, dictated a policy of aggressive recruitment to overcome the minimal disadvantage. The tactics adopted included sparing no expense for transportation, entertainment and the distribution of clothing emblazoned with the FNLA insignia and colors. Meanwhile, military posts were carefully located provocatively close to those of the MPLA, in an attempt to convince the people that the FNLA's tough-looking, well-armed troops offered better protection than did the ragtag MPLA forces.

The MPLA had to respond to this challenge by demonstrating its capacity to defend its supporters against the incursions of this "foreign invader." And so in July [1975], the MPLA mounted against the FNLA posts in Luanda a series of offenses aimed at running them out of town. It is unclear just why the MPLA thought it necessary to antagonize UNITA at the same time (UNITA had taken a neutral stance until then, with its leader, Jonas Savimbi, acting as mediator between Holden Roberto of FNLA and Neto) but it is apparently true that during June and July, the MPLA killed three hundred UNITA troops. . . .

The significance of the MPLA coup d'état, as far as the majority of Luandans were concerned, was not that the transition government had collapsed but rather that the fighting in the city had ceased. The sense of relief was palpable. With the 9 P.M. curfew lifted, people could move about the city without fear of roadblocks or ambushes; it was again possible to visit one's friends and perhaps to move back to an evacuated house. For the MPLA, the expulsion from Luanda of its rivals meant that for the first time since the end of the colonial war it controlled its own tribal area and could therefore proceed unhampered with the implementation of the revolutionary program.

MPLA Doctrine and Program

The central theme of the MPLA's ideology is *poder popular* (people's power). It has always been the MPLA's stated goal to establish an independent Angola based on the premise that the source of power and legitimacy in the government will be the people. In Luanda at least, the institution chosen to transform this revolutionary ideal into practical reality is the *Comissão de Bairro*, or neighborhood committee. Under the Portuguese, these committees operated as local administrative units for the colonial regime; accordingly, they were not particularly responsive to the needs of the African population. The MPLA's innovation has been to recast the committees into popularly elected bodies with a mandate to reorganize and reorient life in the neighborhoods, and at the same time to provide essential social services. In organizational structure, the committees are carbon copies of the MPLA. For example, the committee operating in Sambizanga, an especially large *musseque*, is divided into the following departments: the organization of the masses; information and propaganda; political orientation; supply and production. . . . [However, the] autonomy of operation, the separation, is theoretical. As the departmental breakdown indicates, the committee functions as the local mobilization arm of the MPLA, and while it is difficult to pinpoint exactly the lines of authority, clearly the committee is not an independent entity.

"Mentalization"—Cultural Reeducation

Underlying all mobilization activities is the conviction that the masses must be "mentalized" or reeducated to the task of building a new society. A recurring theme in President Neto's writings is the idea that Portuguese colonialism not only oppressed Angolans politically and economically but culturally; therefore, a political revolution without a corresponding cultural revolution would be a hollow achievement. Neto states: "To construct a country does not mean simply to build houses or open roads; rather it is essentially to transform the mentality of the human being in order that he might consider himself a dignified individual, useful to society." A major objective of "mentalization" is to instill a more cooperative spirit in the approach to work, to motivate workers to labor for the betterment of Angola. The committee's role in this regard is to combine intensive propaganda with organizational guidance in such self-help activities as the improvement of sanitary conditions and the formation of cooperatives.

The Sambizanga food cooperative illustrates the practical way the MPLA is trying simultaneously to educate and mobilize the residents of the neighborhood. Even though the co-op is restricted for the moment to distributing essential foodstuffs: beans, rice, manioc flour, beer and soft drinks, it competes directly with the *cantineiros,* or foodstore owners, who often charge more than the official prices. By shopping at the co-op, members are assured of legal prices and have a chance to strike back at speculators. Thus they are learning that collectively they can improve their lot, which is one aspect of *poder popular.* Of course there have been problems; in spite of the overall success of committee-run co-ops, there have been instances of corruption and some officials landed in jail. The widespread food shortages resulting from the civil war created many opportunities for speculation in the distribution of scarce commodities. However, the MPLA's swift response has restored confidence in its commitment to fair, effective administration.

In a country where the Portuguese kept 90 percent of the population illiterate and where social services for Africans were almost entirely neglected, the committees face an enormous task. Because the needs of the people are so vast, there is no restriction on the scope of their activities—and they are broad indeed. At its most basic, the committee may act as counselor to local residents with personal problems or it may refer them to governmental agencies. Many committees offer working adults evening literacy classes, along with instruction in hygiene, child care, African history and sometimes English. In rare instances, a committee may act as a pressure group to organize opinion on a particular issue —for example, film censorship. I participated in the initial stages of an attempt by the ministry of culture, undertaken in response to the loud outcry of one committee, to establish guidelines for censoring sex and violence in films. I am not sure what impressed me more: the public pressure generated by the committee or the undogmatic, careful attitude with which the MPLA approached the problem. The committees, then, are capable of exerting influence far beyond the boundaries of the neighborhood and there is apparently no limit to the range of their interests.

Productivity: Problems and Bottlenecks

Concern about importing "decadent Western culture" was one manifestation of a moderately puritanical streak in the MPLA, also expressed in exhortations to avoid partying, drunkenness and other unproductive activities. Yet the MPLA's appeals for more work and less play derived more from necessity than from revolutionary fervor; it was a question of survival. While the economic crisis which the MPLA faced as independence approached can in part be blamed on the mass exodus of the Portuguese, the unwillingness of African workers to produce at pre-revolution levels was also an important factor. A possible explanation for their low productivity may be that the workers, conditioned by years of virtual forced labor devoid of any incentive beyond the threat of starvation, had not yet adjusted to their new freedoms as unionized laborers and therefore took advantage of them. Whatever the reason, the consequence was a series of bottlenecks in many sectors of the economy, the most glaring of which was the port of Luanda.

Although they had become the highest paid on the West

African coast, the stevedores . . . [in 1975] handled barely 20 percent of the tonnage of the previous year. Almost the only goods that moved with dispatch through the port were the arms shipments from the Soviet Union and Eastern bloc countries. Ships suffered delays of many months, waiting to unload imports of vital foodstuffs and to take on coffee, a major source of foreign exchange. To combat the wave of wildcat strikes, slowdowns and work stoppages, in the main unjustified, the MPLA undertook a vigorous propaganda campaign urging workers to set aside their grievances for the greater good of the new Angola. Slogans such as: "To produce is to resist" and "There is no revolution without production" bombarded the city from posters, newspapers, radio and television, while the MPLA leaders hammered away at the theme in mass rallies.

Fostering Political Consciousness

Television, very much in the experimental stage when I left Angola . . . [in November 1975] will undoubtedly be employed more extensively as a propaganda medium. Sets were distributed to the committees when daily programs began in October, an indication that the MPLA plans to exploit TV as far as possible. The programs I saw consisted mainly of news reports, heavily laced with diatribes against the FNLA/UNITA coalition and supplemented by an occasional documentary on African peoples and culture. Presumably, systematic educational and propagandistic programming will in time become standard fare, but the first night of Angolan television will be hard to surpass—*Viva Zapata* with Marlon Brando and Anthony Quinn was shown, complete with commentary on the development of a political consciousness among the Mexican peasants and its relevance to the Angolan revolution.

It is hard to judge how effective the MPLA's "mentalization" campaign has been so far. I found the average Luandan surprisingly sophisticated in the use of MPLA political rhetoric and always willing to discuss the Angolan situation, particularly with foreigners. Hitchhikers, upon learning that

I was an American, would invariably challenge me to justify "US imperialist" activity in Angola. In discussions with MPLA political commissars who are responsible for the indoctrination of recruits to the FAPLA [People's Liberation Armed Forces] (the military wing of the MPLA), I was especially impressed by how little their revolutionary dogma blinded them to the realities of the civil war. They readily acknowledged and sought to overcome tribal resistance to their movement in such regions as Cabinda, where they eventually succeeded in earning the respect if not the love of the Cabindans. The FNLA soldiers, on the other hand, were led to believe that Luandans would welcome them as conquering heroes; when instead they encountered hostility, they quickly became demoralized.

Tribal Divisions Versus a Unified Nation

Yet these admittedly superficial observations should not suggest that the MPLA will easily overcome tribal divisions and forge a unified Angola in the near future. On the contrary, it is as yet by no means in complete control of even its own supporters, and much will depend upon its ability to discipline its militants, specifically the FAPLA and the local militia, to the end of winning the confidence of other tribal groups. In August . . . [1975] an incident that occurred in Luanda gave the MPLA a chance to demonstrate its commitment to strict discipline. At the height of the battle for Luanda in July, the MPLA had hastily armed neighborhood defense forces to help drive the FNLA from the city. After the battle, these ill-trained militia retained their weapons and began a rampage of looting in the *musseques*. Six members of a defense force led by a FAPLA commander named Bom dos Boms (a *nom de guerre* [war name] meaning, literally, the good of the good ones) who had been a guerrilla since 1959, massacred eleven men, women and children after a Saturday night spree. The following Wednesday the MPLA staged a public trial and invited the crowd to render the verdict. Unimpressed by the defendants' testimony, the crowd shouted "guilty." An ex-

cadres. About fifty miles from the Zambian border we came upon the outer rim of the complex network of UNITA base areas and villages which sprawls over half the territory of Angola.

Neto continually dismisses the guerrillas as a few scattered bands of traitors and thieves. Around the campfires at night the guerrillas listen with mingled amusement and irritation to the broadcasts from Luanda which report their imminent extinction. These same broadcasts exhort the local farmers to increase their food production: there is a chronic food shortage in Angola. But in the small villages of thatched huts with conical straw roofs, the elderly men and women who would bring us river water in gourds complained to us of MPLA raids on their crops and cattle. Many villagers have been forced to move four or five times in . . . [a] few months to avoid harassment by Cuban and MPLA troops.

Walking fifty miles a day over parched landscape with insufficient food and water under a blinding sun tends to bring political abstractions about freedom and independence into touch with reality. It is difficult for Westerners to comprehend this society being forged in the African bush from a dislocated population of city refugees and rural villagers. Ninety percent of Angola's six million people lived in rural areas before the civil war. Roughly one quarter of that population is now scattered in neighboring countries. Huambo, formerly a city of 250,000, today has fewer than 50,000 inhabitants. A missionary who returned there recently reported that the former citizens have deserted the city.

> You can see the fires at night surrounding the city [he said]. I preached there for years and never suspected that the residents would join any armed resistance. But they are out there, on the hillsides, in the camps waiting . . . waiting perhaps for the day they may retake the city.

What is left of the city is currently governed by a Cuban general. In the rural areas controlled by UNITA, the dislocation of Angola's society is evident in poignant vignettes.

You run across extraordinary sights. A refugee from the city, now eating masonge, a gruel made from pounded maize, and picking the bones of a lean stewed chicken, sits at a table hewn from logs but draped with a white linen tablecloth. Some of the city people cannot adjust to life in the bush. Many, for lack of food and medicine, or because they are old or lack the necessary resilience, drift over the borders into exile in Zaïre or Zambia.

In a handwritten letter we received from Savimbi, he wrote:

> We have thousands and thousands of people in the bush and they are not prepared to go back to the villages, the towns, and the cities which the MPLA control. Their plight is serious. We have to feed them. We think their presence as important as the armed resistance because the popular resistance to the Cubans is found among these people.

The influx of city dwellers into the UNITA camps has helped eliminate a perennial African problem—how to convey to the people an idea of nationhood. We met Angolans from the distant coastal cities of Lobito, Benguela, Moçamedes, and Luanda as well as from nearby Serpa Pinto, Luso, and Gago Coutinho. The residents of Freeland, old and new, perceive themselves as exiles in their own land.

Cubans: The New Colonialists?

And the principal enemy is the foreign invader—the Cubans, considered by many Angolans as the new colonialists. In an interview at his headquarters in central Angola during the last week in October, Jonas Savimbi remarked on UNITA's newfound optimism:

> The Cubans never fought anywhere. What they call their battle for liberation from the hills of Sierra Maestra to Batista's palace was really a picnic. The Portuguese knew how to exploit the terrain, the natural conditions, and the native population. The Cubans do none of these; instead they fight the people. Once they started to fight the people, they spelled their own defeat.

UNITA leaders and troops admire the Portuguese as soldiers, but even so, they are quick to point out, Portugal was for four centuries held to the coastal areas of Angola. Not until the 1930s did they move inland, and even then a third of the country always remained beyond their effective control. With a force four times the size of the present Cuban contingent, they were never able to wipe out a less well-trained and less well-armed guerrilla opposition.

The MPLA Establishment

Yet, on the surface everything would seem to be going Neto's way. Internationally, Neto's Cuban-backed government with its Soviet arsenal has, since last February [1976] been recognized by the OAU [Organization of African Unity], the European Economic Community, the United Nations, and every country in the world except the United States and China. In April the MPLA reached an agreement with South Africa, their former enemy. If South Africa doesn't interfere in the civil war and aids, directly or indirectly, the stability of the Luanda regime, the MPLA will guarantee the security of the South African interests in the Cunene dam project and in the diamond mines in the Lunda district of northeastern Angola. In the north, the Gulf Oil Company, which had put its royalties in escrow during the civil war, is now paying them into Neto's treasury, providing roughly 60 percent of Angola's current foreign revenues.

Militarily, UNITA is pitted against a force of at least 15,000 Cubans, an equal number of MPLA troops, 3,000 mercenaries from Katanga province in Zaïre, and 3,000 Soviet-trained SWAPO [South West African People's Organization] guerrillas. (SWAPO is the group spearheading the liberation movement in South West Africa.) The Cuban and government troops are armed with Soviet tanks and MiGs, surface-to-surface missiles, and helicopters. Against this force, UNITA has a reported 15,000 guerrillas, armed with a wild array of weapons—Russian, Chinese, American, British, French, Czech—three radio transmitters, and, at last count, thirty-four donkeys.

It is not difficult to see in the Angolan military situation parallels with Indochina, where American troops—and the French before them—held the towns and the cities, and the guerrillas operated from fluid bases in the bush, striking out at convoys, tearing up railway links, and moving at night.

The Guerrilla War

The situation around Huambo is typical of UNITA's overall strategy. The guerrillas in the area have mined major supply routes into the city and now conduct ambushes on Cuban-MPLA convoys transporting military equipment and supplies to garrisons there. On the November 11 anniversary of Angola's supposed independence, UNITA guerrillas blew up two trains in the middle of the city. In many cases elsewhere in southern and central Angola, we found UNITA encampments only a few miles from the isolated small towns held by Cuban and MPLA outposts. For example, there are eleven UNITA base areas, with a thousand or so guerrillas and many more refugees and villagers, encircling the town of Muie. To reach the town, traffic must now pass through guerrilla-held locations and checkpoints. The UNITA camps—usually in clusters of five or six, together forming a base—consist of numerous roughly constructed thatched huts with long bark strips marking the camps' perimeters. We were not allowed to walk unaccompanied outside the perimeters because the guerrillas have placed land mines in the surrounding bush.

To reinforce their garrisons, the Cubans run armored convoys through guerrilla-held areas. They use the MPLA soldiers as "gun flesh" who lead the way to make sure the roads are clear and to draw guerrilla fire away from the armored divisions. The Cuban forces in these garrisons generally remain inside the city limits, leaving the MPLA soldiers to conduct search-and-destroy missions that often take a greater toll of villagers and farmers than of UNITA guerrillas. . . .

[Between June 1976 and the beginning of 1977] there have been five major coordinated military efforts to dislodge

UNITA. . . . Cuban and government forces have swept from Andulo in central Angola across Serpa Pinto in southern Angola down to the provinces of Huila and Cuando Cubango. At times as many as 25,000 troops, supported by airborne assault divisions, armored cars, and tanks, have been engaged in these widespread offensives. The last of these, which began in southern Angola . . . [in] September [1976], was viewed as a final concerted effort to destroy UNITA's military effectiveness or, failing this, to eliminate its base of political support. The offensive ended up destroying many villages and slaughtering the cattle of the Cuanhamas and Ovambo tribes who, along with the Ovimbundu people, are the major meat and poultry producers in Angola. It also resulted in the flight into South West Africa of another ten thousand refugees. In late November, failing to achieve their goals, Cuban and government troops with their allies began a "strategic retreat" to the MPLA's northern strongholds.

According to UNITA figures—which other military intelligence sources tend to substantiate— . . . [these] eight months of fighting have resulted in over 2,500 Cuban and MPLA casualties, and the loss of a substantial number of Soviet helicopters and tanks. In addition, Cuban soldiers have been defecting to Congo-Brazzaville and Zambia. On December 21 [1976], 142 Cuban soldiers drove their military vehicles across the border into Zambia and requested asylum.

When we were transported back across the border by an "underground railway" manned by refugees living in another land, we reentered a world where political rhetoric camouflages the harsh realities of the Angolan situation. In the realm of valued public-relations campaigns, UNITA is powerless and without organization. But the MPLA argument that Angola lacks the proper technological expertise or is still struggling to mend the ravages of the civil war cannot account for the paralysis of Angola's economy and the inability of the Luanda government to muster public support. The Benguela Railway, despite government claims about its impending reopening, remains closed to commercial traffic to Zaïre and Zambia. Only military traffic sporadically inches its way toward Angola's heartlands. Periodic sabotage by UNITA guerrillas keeps the Benguela effectively closed. Construction on the hydroelectric projects in the south has been suspended because of continued military activity. The coffee crop in the northwestern regions has been destroyed by the FNLA who have in recent months reemerged as an active guerrilla force. Only 20 percent of . . . [the 1976] crop, mostly from stored supplies, will be exported. Ironically, more than three thousand Cuban troops are currently engaged in protecting Gulf Oil operations in Cabinda from renewed guerrilla activity in the province. According to US officials, only the oil operations and the main city of Cabinda remain under the control of the Luanda government. In central and southern Angola the people's refusal to ship their food products to government markets has resulted in widespread starvation and retaliatory actions against the recalcitrant farmers and cattle-raisers. Dried fish is currently the only source of protein for people under the government's control. Dock strikes and rampant absenteeism in factories have drastically lowered productivity.

Behind the media curtain, Angola is not a country grappling with the difficult problems of development but a nation in resistance. UNITA and, to a lesser degree, the other Angolan groups are fighting a guerrilla war according to the maxims of Mao, with the guerrilla fish swimming in the friendly waters of a receptive population. For this other Angola, the war for liberation has not ended.

SOMALIA: CHANGING OF THE GUARD [5]

It was hardly a dignified leave-taking. A gaggle of Russians, the first of many such groups to run the same gauntlet . . . [in November 1977], gathered in the hot, squalid main

      [5] Article entitled "Russians, Go Home!" *Time.* 110:48. N. 28, '77. Reprinted by permission from *Time,* the weekly newsmagazine; Copyright Time Inc. 1977.

hall of Mogadishu airport to await an Aeroflot flight to Aden. [Mogadishu, the capital of Somalia, is a seaport on the Indian Ocean; Aden, the capital of the People's Democratic Republic of Yemen, is a port on the Gulf of Aden.] Somali customs officials, who normally give departing passengers a bored wave-through, set upon the sweating travelers with malicious grins, demanding that they open every suitcase for an item-by-item inspection. At the airport bar, quarrels broke out as the bartender doubled the price of Cokes. A Western TV cameraman recording the pandemonium took an elbow in the ribs from an incensed Russian.

Thus planeload by sweltering planeload did the remaining 1,500 Soviet personnel and some 45 Cuban comrades depart Somalia, one of the Kremlin's oldest foreign-aid footholds in black Africa. As one group was preparing to leave, an American Air Force 707 landed, bearing a US congressional delegation on its way to lunch with Somali President Mohamed Siad Barre. The delegation's long-scheduled arrival was sheer coincidence, to be sure, but the symbolism was unmistakable.

As had been predicted, the Somalis were throwing the Russians out. They denounced their three-year-old friendship treaty with the Soviet Union, and they asked the Russians to vacate the Soviet-built naval base at the Somali port of Berbera on the Gulf of Aden. Soviet military and civilian advisers were ordered to get out of the country on a week's notice, leaving just seven USSR embassy employees in Mogadishu—the exact size of the Somali embassy staff in Moscow. Simultaneously, the Somalis broke off diplomatic relations with Cuba.

The break was all but inevitable in view of the massive support that Moscow and Havana have been sending to Ethiopia, the Somalis' enemy. The Somalis had known for at least three years that the Kremlin, for all its protestations of good intentions toward Somalia, was forging new ties with Addis Ababa [Ethiopia]. Then war broke out in Ethiopia's Ogaden desert . . . [in July 1977] between Ethiopian forces and the ethnic Somalis who live there; the insurgents are backed and armed by Mogadishu. After that, the Somalis quickly realized that, as one official puts it, "our brothers were being killed by bullets supplied by the people who said they were our friends."

The Soviets had been aiding Somalia ever since the early 1960s. helping to make it one of the best-armed nations in Africa, with a 22,000-man army, three MiG-equipped fighter squadrons and six tank battalions. Until the mid-1970s Ethiopia, under the late Emperor Haile Selassie, received substantial aid and arms from the United States. But after the emperor's overthrow in 1974 by a leftist junta, Addis Ababa's relations with the United States cooled. Despite their ties to Somalia, the Russians saw a chance to establish a presence in Ethiopia, which is almost ten times as populous as Somalia and whose ancient feudal society might prove more receptive to Soviet socialism over the long run than Muslim Somalia had been. Many observers think Moscow diplomats genuinely believed they could continue to have it two ways: maintaining close ties with both Mogadishu and Addis Ababa while tilting toward Ethiopia in the current war.

If so, they underestimated the fiercely independent Somalis. In late August, Barre made his final trip to Moscow, where he was snubbed by Soviet President Leonid Brezhnev and was refused the heavy weapons he sought. Barre then visited Saudi Arabia, whose leaders had been trying to woo him away from Moscow for at least three years as part of their anti-Communist strategy to reinforce moderate regimes along the Red Sea and on the Horn of Africa [Somalia and Ethiopia]. Barre came away from Jeddah with a reported promise of $300 million; in return, he presumably promised the Saudis that he would get rid of the Russians in his own good time.

The result so far is something of a geopolitical standoff. The Soviets have lost their primary Indian Ocean naval facility, but can probably find some kind of alternative—possibly on Ethiopia's Red Sea coastline. They have ex-

the price. I was born in freedom, and I know the difference."

CUBA: DEVELOPMENT AND ITS PROBLEMS [2]

The contrasts of Cuba are as dazzling as the Caribbean. Oxen still plow fields where billboards proclaim that "the future belongs to socialism," and horsemen ride down roads past model agricultural communities with a television set in every home and a theater playing Bulgarian movies.

The Havana suburbs are a Co-op City [huge high-rise apartment complex in the North Bronx] done in pastels, while five miles away *campesinos* [peasants] still live in thatched-roof huts. And the manager of a state collective farm, patterned on the Soviet model, turns out to be a former New York City resident who can name every baseball player on the roster of the 1934 Boston Braves.

Yet beneath the diversity and incongruities of this island economy, equivalent in productive capacity to Chile, or Colombia, lie two fundamental realities: dedication to socialism and dependence on sugar.

Twenty years after Fidel Castro began his struggle in the Sierra Maestra, Cuba is the only Western Hemisphere nation set firmly in the Socialist mold. More than one quarter of the land is still in private hands, but virtually all commerce and industry is directed by the state, down to the ice cream shops off the Malecon, the scenic ocean drive along the north shore of Havana.

The economy as a whole is guided by the centralized planning and bureaucratic management typical of Eastern Europe. And largely because of the American economic embargo, imposed in 1962, about 70 percent of Cuban trade, which totaled $6.48 billion . . . [in 1976], is with the Socialist countries. This is roughly the same proportion as the

[2] From an article entitled "The Cuban Economy: How It Works," by Ann Crittenden, staff reporter. New York *Times*. sec III, p 1+. D. 18, '77. © 1977 by The New York Times Company. Reprinted by permission.

United States' share of Cuban trade before the embargo.

The bulk of that trade was, and is, in sugar. Cuba, the world's largest sugar exporter, remains a predominantly rural, one-crop economy, dependent on the cane fields for fully 86 percent of its foreign earnings. Roughly 50 percent of the population of nearly 10 million still works in agriculture, compared with 5 percent in the United States. The Cubans are working hard to mechanize the sugar harvest and release labor for other tasks, but after years of experimentation they are resigned to the fact that sugar is still their lifeblood.

Sweet and Sour

That lesson was driven home harshly in the mid-1970s, when world sugar prices swung radically from more than 60 cents a pound in 1974 to 7 cents . . . [in 1976]. Though roughly 60 percent of the annual harvest of 5 to 6 billion tons is sold to the Socialist countries at fixed (and currently above-market) rates, the runup in 1974 gave Cuba its first hard-currency trade surplus in years and permitted a surge of imports from the West.

When the price swung down again, however, imports had to be brutally slashed, and this year [1977] they will be down to about half the 1975 level, according to Lawrence Theriot of the [US] Commerce Department, an authority on the Cuban economy. The cutback forced a scaling back of production goals in general and a deferral of plans for the development of light industry in particular. According to Mr. Theriot, investment in the basic infrastructure such as roads and power generation is being maintained through the trade with Eastern Europe.

Most analysts believe that the Cuban economy hit bottom last year and has now begun to recover, partly because of the more modest planning goals. Moreover, the International Sugar Agreement . . . [of October 1977] will at least guarantee that the international price of sugar will rise to a floor level of 11 cents a pound within the next couple of years. (A ceiling, of 21 cents, was also set.) As a result, Cuba, with a quota of 2.5 million tons to sell in the free market, stands to earn at least $600 million in foreign exchange by 1980.

Russian Subsidies, Western Debts

Nevertheless, this will not be enough in the near term to free the country from its heavy dependence on the Soviet Union. According to a detailed analysis of the Cuban economy prepared this year by the Business International Corporation, a business advisory and publishing company, Cuba has received more aid from the Soviet Union than any other Latin American nation has received from any source. The total Cuban debt to the Soviet Union is estimated at $4.8 billion. When the purchase of Cuban sugar and nickel at above-market prices and the sale of oil at below-market prices are taken into account, the accumulated Soviet subsidy of Cuba comes to some $8 billion.

Moreover, according to US government data, in the last two years the Russians have funneled more than $700 million of their sugar payments to the island in hard currency. And in an agreement signed in 1976, the Russians reportedly promised to transact 25 percent of future sugar sales in hard currency. In addition to its Soviet debt, Cuba by the end of last year also owed an estimated $1.3 billion to Western banks, largely for trade credits. . . .

US Détente

One of the few alternatives to Cuba's foreign-exchange bind is a renewal of trade with the United States, which before the Cuban revolution took almost 60 percent of the island's sugar exports. The Cubans estimate that the 1978 harvest will come to more than 7 million tons, and they are shooting for 8 to 8.5 million tons by 1980. They frankly hope to sell that surplus in the United States. . . .

This wish explains much of the Cuban interest in restoring normal relations with the United States. Recently there have been friendly receptions for hundreds of American businessmen and members of Congress in Havana. They have been lodged in luxurious hotels . . . , deluged with rum and given lengthy Cuban shopping lists.

The Cubans are particularly interested in buying American agribusiness equipment and technology, capital equipment, computers, rice and medicine. In a major speech . . . [in September 1977], President Castro warned that, if trade resumes, Cuba would not spend its scarce resources on "junk and trinkets," meaning imported consumer goods. . . . "The needs we did have for American equipment practically don't exist any more" . . . [said Marcelo Fernandez Font, Cuba's minister of foreign trade]. "We've either adapted to other technologies or the equipment we had has become completely obsolete."

The trade ministry has told the American government that, if the embargo were lifted next year, the United States could garner as much as 30 percent of Cuba's trade with the West, or $300 million to $350 million in the first year. "That amount is a starting point, not a ceiling," said Mr. Fernandez.

Even with optimistic assumptions, however, about Cuban earnings from nickel, seafood, citrus, tobacco and tourism—Cuba's only significant exports apart from sugar— Mr. Theriot of the Commerce Department sees a maximum of $320 million in American exports to Cuba by 1981. Total United States exports last year were $115 billion.

In any event, an immediate lifting of the embargo seems problematic, in view of the two nations' . . . dispute over the presence of Cuban troops in Angola. Another serious sticking point is the $1.8 billion in claims for expropriated assets in Cuba, largely in the public services and the sugar, oil and food-processing industries.

Cuba, which has paid off companies in other foreign countries when their governments recognized the Castro government, says it won't talk about the claims until the embargo is lifted; the United States has said it won't lift the embargo until the claims are settled. A Joint Corporate Committee on Cuban Claims, made up of fifty American companies, including Bordens, United Brands, Bangor

Punta and Lone Star Industries, is lobbying against any trade or diplomatic relations before the claims are settled.

Social Investment of Government Funds: Health, Education, Welfare

However significant the debate over restoring trade with the United States, the basic thrust of Cuba's economic planning is what is known in development circles as "basic human needs": education, health and housing. The government has poured much of its resources into social investment, often with dramatic results.

In 1959, when the Batista government fell, rural illiteracy was 43 percent; today the nationwide rate is 22 percent. Of the country people who went to school, 88 percent had not passed the third grade; now the average is sixth grade. Rural per capita income was less than $100; estimates of the average now run from $550 to $850 in a country where education and health care are free, rents by law can be no higher than 10 percent of income, basic foods are sold at 1965 prices and public transportation and telephones cost next to nothing. As a result of the various social programs, life expectancy at birth is now 70 years, compared with 71 in the United States, 63 in Mexico and 61 in Brazil.

In an interview, President Castro left no doubt that education, which absorbs more than 7 percent of Cuba's gross national product, is a top priority. Cuba lost many of its professional workers in the migration of the 1960s, including half its doctors. With obvious gusto, Mr. Castro rattled off figures: 880,000 students in secondary schools, up from . . . [the number enrolled] before the revolution; 130,000 university student, up from 115,000, and a medical school class of 3,500 . . . [in 1977].

The plan is to have all the secondary students eventually enrolled in work-study programs, spending half their time at each, both to teach them respect for labor and to help defray the costs of their education. "We don't want a society of intellectuals," Mr. Castro declared.

The nation's fundamental problem, an assistant to Mr. Castro said recently, is food. Cuba, he pointed out, has the same population density in relation to arable land as China. Staples such as rice, beans, meat and coffee are strictly rationed in Cuba (as is clothing).

Meat, for example, is limited to twelve ounces per person every nine days, although fish is free of rationing. A recent visit to a Havana supermarket showed little more than the basic necessities and, to American eyes, an extremely limited supply of fresh fruit and vegetables.

Cuban economists say that the emphasis in food production is now on fresh produce and dairy products. At a state dairy farm in Matanzas province, east of Havana, officials claimed that milk production had increased sharply, partly because of the development of a new breed of cattle, the F-2, a cross between the Holstein and the Brahmin. This animal's yield is only about half that of the best milk cow in the United States, however.

The Consumer: Earning and Spending

The emphasis on productive investment in Cuba, rather than consumption, has produced a severe liquidity problem. Families have relatively high incomes, particularly with more and more women working, but little they can spend their money on. The state tries to siphon off some of the excess cash by allowing unrationed purchases of expensive, Cuban-made luxuries such as rum and tobacco. And there is talk of eventually permitting the purchase of private houses as a means of sopping up some of the money in circulation.

Another way to spend excess cash is to dine out. Havana seems to be full of distinctly prerevolutionary restaurants packed with Cubans. At the Floredita, an old favorite of Ernest Hemingway's where the waiters are formally attired, a lobster dinner for five costs about $185.

Workers on the state farms now being organized all over Cuba are given furnished houses, including television sets, when they turn their small land holdings over to the collective, where they work a forty-four-hour week for a salary. A housing project for the state dairy farm, called the Triunvirate, included a school and playgrounds, shops and a movie theater for the 1,600 people living there.

The plan is for the entire countryside to be organized in this fashion, eliminating the traditional isolation and poverty of rural life. The notion is an old Marxist one, but it is also an attempt to prevent the massive rural-to-urban migrations that have plagued other twentieth-century societies. The strategy seems to be working: Havana is virtually the only major city in Latin America that is not surrounded by a ring of fetid slums.

The Cubans are not hesitant about acknowledging that, to induce the rural workers to stay down on the farm, they have offered an array of material incentives, including more abundant food than exists in Havana. Material incentives are held out for other workers as well. Tickets to the Tropicana nightclub, a week's vacation at Varadero Beach and a top spot on the waiting list for a new apartment or an electric appliance are among the spurs to greater productivity.

After the failure in the 1960s to create a new economic man, motivated by purely moral incentives, an Economic Management and Planning System was introduced. It is moving the management of factories, state farms and other institutions toward an entrepreneurial structure. Henceforth administrators will be under pressure to generate a surplus of earnings over costs, which they can choose to invest in the enterprise, distribute to the workers or put into social improvements, such as day-care centers or recreational facilities.

Explaining this reform, modeled on methods tried elsewhere in the Socialist world, José Llanusa, the head of the state dairy farm, said: "In the transitional stage from one kind of society to another, you have to distinguish between the worker who is efficient and the one who isn't. Of course, that distinction cannot include the rights of all families to education, health care and basic services."

CHILE: A STUDY IN COUNTERREVOLUTION [3]

During its three stormy years Chile's Allende regime was often described as "a decisive test case," though there was some confusion about what precisely was being tested.

Salvador Allende Gossens was a professed "revolutionary Marxist." His avowed objective was the revolutionary transformation of his nation according to the Marxist prescription: the elimination of private property in the means of production—mines, factories, transport, banks, land holdings of any size, etc. He sometimes declared himself to be a "Communist," but he was not an avowed member of the Communist party, and his exact relation to the party is a matter of dispute. In economic and social policy, Allende was well to the left of social democracy, but he nevertheless insisted that he was a democrat, and that he aimed to bring about the Marxist revolution through the democratic process.

The Non-Communist Perspective:
A Test of Parliamentary Socialism

Allende was chosen president in 1970 by a process that was peaceful and in accord with Chile's constitution, though flawed from the standpoint of democratic legitimacy by the fact that he had won only 34 percent of the popular vote. His government was based politically on a "popular union" of his own small revolutionary Socialist party, the official (Moscow) Communist party, the leftist faction of the Christian Democrats and fringe groups. This coalition failed to win a majority in the 1972 legislative election.

What the Allende episode was testing, according to the non-Communist formulation, was whether a nation could and would shift to a Marxist system by peaceful, democratic means. The meaning of "Marxist" was left vague. Presumably it meant something beyond the welfarist mixed socialism that is endemic in our day.

[3] Article entitled "The Chilean Lessons: The Protracted Conflict," by James Burnham, a staff editor. *National Review*. 26:1094. S. 27, '74. Reprinted by permission.

Insofar as the episode was a test, the answer it supplied was no, but the test was blurred. Allende's democratic credentials were never in complete order. From almost the day he took office, there was extralegal violence: beginning with the factory, office, and land seizures by left extremists, later spreading to antirevolutionary elements of the population, and culminating in the counterrevolutionary coup of the military junta.

The Communist Analysis: A Transitional Form of Government

The Communists formulate their analysis within a different framework. Their fixed long-term objective is the conquest of a monopoly of power. A coalition government is an advanced form of "united front." Communists enter an electoral or governmental coalition, or any other united front, as a maneuver in their struggle for power. Participation in the united front gives them a favorable position from which to undermine the bourgeois social and political structure, to combat anti-Communist parties and leaders, and to gain access to the followers of their partners (i.e., victims) in the front.

For the Communists, the Allende government was a transitional, pre-revolutionary political formation on the Communist road to power. The democratic trappings were only incidental, and violence somewhere along the line was taken for granted. If the Communists did not themselves initiate violence, their doctrine—which the Chilean evidence gives them no reason to revise—teaches that the ruling class never gives up peacefully. From their standpoint, things turned out badly in Chile, at least for the time being: the transition ended with the counterrevolution instead of the revolution in the saddle.

The Lessons of Chile

What went wrong?

This past summer [1974] the Soviet press, *World Marxist Review*, and other Communist theoretical journals have been publishing articles on the Chilean episode by Soviet leaders—among them Boris Ponomarev and N. Kudachkin (both with special responsibilities for Communist parties in non-Communist countries) and the theoretician A. Sobolev—thus emphasizing the importance of Chile for international Communist strategy.

According to the approved analysis, the following are among the major factors that led to the Communist setback in Chile:

1. The counterrevolutionary press was not quickly enough muzzled. Chile's influential conservative paper, *El Mercurio,* is cited for its role in wrecking the Allende regime.

2. The Allende government moved too slowly on both the political and economic fronts, thus giving the counterrevolution time to prepare it forces.

3. The Chilean Communists failed to push Allende into speedy nationalization of private business without compensation.

4. The Chilean Communists did not go far and fast enough in creating grass roots organizations of workers and peasants (i.e., soviets) under Communist control which could act as an extralegal power apparatus.

5. The adventurous and disorganized seizures of farms and some factories by ultraleft Maoists and Trotskyites antagonized potential sympathizers and aroused the reactionary elements.

6. Communist penetration of the armed forces, though considerable, was not sufficient to deter the coup by the higher military echelons.

Preventive Measures

The analysis is thus not theoretical but strategic and tactical. Local Communists are being told to revise their manuals for dealing with a Chile-type situation if it arises or can be made to arise in their country. The message is marked Urgent, since the Communist leaders see two, three, many Chiles looming on the near historical horizon. One, in fact, is already in motion in Portugal, and there the lessons drawn from Chile are being put to vigorous use. Only one Portuguese newspaper still remains out of Communist or allied leftist control; Communist infiltration of the armed forces has gone deeper than it ever achieved in Chile, and the Communists have virtually no organized opposition in their penetration of the trade unions. Spain and Greece are on the candidate list. The early September demand of the Italian Communist party to be included in the governmental coalition was an attempt to swing Italy onto the Chilean road. Even France, where this spring the presidential candidate of the united front lost by only a percentage point, is among the possibles.

IV. EUROCOMMUNISM

EDITOR'S INTRODUCTION

Although Communist parties are active throughout Europe, discussions of Eurocommunism generally center on the three countries whose parties are strongest or whose leaders are most vocal: Italy, France, and Spain. In none of these countries can the Communist party command a majority; in none does it yet have the largest plurality. In each, however, the Communists are strong enough to gain a share of national power through coalitions.

Since none of these countries has a Communist government, it is not surprising that their Communist parties disavow affiliation with the USSR or that they are on the defensive to prove their disavowal is not a tactical pronouncement. Criticism of the USSR by European Communist leaders has been voiced increasingly in recent years. Perhaps the strongest expression is to be found in *Eurocommunism and the State,* by Santiago Carrillo, head of Spain's recently legalized Communist party, whose barbs have on several occasions drawn bitter criticism in the Soviet weekly *New Times.*

The second controversial issue is the Eurocommunists' acceptance of democratic parliamentary procedures in principle and not as a temporary stratagem for gaining power. Here they must contend with criticisms that they practice "democratic centralism," in which intraparty discussion is permitted only while policy is being shaped: Once a decision has been made, the minority must submit; protest is met with expulsion.

The articles in this section examine the history, claims, and credibility of Eurocommunism. British author Edward Crankshaw sees a positive political role for the Eurocommunist program as a foil to both Moscow-led communism and a resurgent right-wing extremism.

Political scientist Charles Gati, in the next article, taken from *Foreign Affairs*, discusses precursors of Eurocommunism and the promises broken and kept by various Communist parties; his main interest is the possible impact of Western European communism on Eastern Europe. The third article, from *Time* magazine, presents brief excerpts from Carrillo's book.

In the concluding articles Michael Ledeen, writing in *Commentary*, and Jean-François Revel, writing in *Foreign Affairs*, take more skeptical positions. Ledeen concentrates on press coverage of Eurocommunism. Revel stresses differences in Eurocommunist coalitions, the tradition of a non-Communist Left, and the disputes between Socialists and Communists that were one factor in their defeat at the polls in France in March 1978.

EUROPE'S REDS: TROUBLE FOR MOSCOW [1]

Change in the Communist world is so slow that only the specialist's eye can usually make it out. It goes on all the same, though as a rule, and for quite long periods, hidden from the outside view.

Once in a while, there is an earthquake that brings about a radical change, even though it may take the outside world years to believe the evidence of its own eyes. A Yugoslav Communist called Tito, who is also a patriot and a natural leader in his own right, throws down the gauntlet to Stalin, refusing to be bossed about, and, amazingly, survives—thus exploding forever the illusion that Soviet power is limitless (1948). Mao Tse-tung leads his Chinese Communists to victory in the teeth of Stalin's disapproval and establishes what must inevitably become a rival power base to Moscow (1949).

[1] From an article by Edward Crankshaw, well-known British writer on Russian affairs, author of *The Shadow of the Winter Palace*. New York *Times Magazine*. p 18–20+. F. 12, '78. © 1978 by The New York Times Company. Reprinted by permission.

Stalin dies (1953), and his death sets off a chain reaction, beginning with the abandonment of wholesale terror inside the Soviet Union and continuing to this day.

The latest manifestation of this chain reaction is the emergence of a phenomenon called Eurocommunism, and, as usual, a certain kind of skeptic insists that it does not mean a thing, that communism is what it always has been and always will be, that any changes in the professed beliefs or goals of any Communist party are nothing but deception. Unenlightened skepticism is as dangerous as and much sillier than exaggerated credulity: There are still people who believe that the great quarrel between Russia and China is not real. We should not make the same sort of mistake about the Eurocommunists.

Eurocommunism

The term *Eurocommunism* is now used to include all those Western European Communist parties that have come to reject total subservience to Moscow. This, as far as I can discover, means *all* the Western European parties, though one or two, like the British Communist party, have split, with a minority group setting itself up as the repository of the true faith, wholly loyal to Moscow. But Eurocommunism implies more than simple refusal to obey the Kremlin's orders blindly and in all particulars. If this were all, then Marshal Tito would be a Eurocommunist, but he is not. So would Nicolae Ceausescu of Rumania, who most decidedly is not. Certainly Eurocommunism includes a strong element of nationalism, but its really distinguishing feature is that it stands for the victory of Marxism by parliamentary means and, furthermore (at least in some cases), the throwing overboard of the very idea of the dictatorship of the proletariat —i.e., the dictatorship of the innermost circle of the Communist party.

This gives the Russians much pain. But the interesting thing is that although the term *Eurocommunism* was invented only two or three years ago, and has become fashionable over the past year, and although the conflict between

Moscow and the Eurocommunists was dramatized conspicuously for all to see only [in] June, [1977] in the historic clash between the Kremlin and the Spanish Communist leader Santiago Carrillo, the Russians have been wrestling with it in vain for the last twenty years. It is no sudden growth. And it is here to stay.

Eurocommunists: Natural Traditions and Differences

The decision to seek power not through violent revolution but openly, by parliamentary means, by persuasion and maneuver, is important for the time being only in those countries that have strong Communist parties—that is, in Italy and France. Obviously, the prospect of Communist parties in NATO countries attaining even a share in government, let alone control of it, is bound to alarm the more nervous spirits in the West, regardless of the fact that there have [long] been Communists in the Icelandic cabinet. . . .

The immediate worry over France has been relieved by the collapse of the electoral alliance among French Socialists, radicals and Communists, a bonus for [President] Giscard d'Estaing. The breakdown may inject new vitality into the moderate Socialists, but it is certainly not the end of the Communist party's attempt to work its way to power in France, as in other West European countries, by what it likes to call parliamentary means. It is obvious that Georges Marchais, the French Communist leader, has himself forced the break for tactical reasons, almost certainly because he has decided that his Communists are not yet strong enough to dominate any coalition. Making a virtue of necessity, he has reverted to his old line of rather bad-tempered intransigence.

The Communists in Italy, on the other hand, have recently become much more demanding. Instead of continuing to lend their support to Giulio Andreotti and his Christian Democratic Party, they precipitated a government crisis by insisting on cabinet representation. Now Enrico Berlinguer declares that rather than call a general election, the Communists should be invited to form a government. [In July 1978 the Christian Democrats and the Communists agreed on the choice of Socialist Sandro Pertini for the presidency.—Ed.]

It is still too early to draw conclusions from these developments. What seems to me certain is that the first major rift in the image of reconciliation between the Socialists and Communists of Western Europe cannot possibly be seen as the end of a process that has struck deep roots. It is no more than a check, a check useful and salutary to use if only because it brings home certain valuable lessons.

First, we are reminded how hard it is for Communists to change their spots, even when they are trying. But perhaps the most important point, which we are forever forgetting, is that no two Communist parties are alike. Thus, for decades, the French Communist party has been a byword for intransigence and suspicious secretiveness. Exhibiting in its relations with other Communist parties (to say nothing of the non-Communist world) something of that touchy, chauvinistic disdain seen at its most extreme in de Gaulle, it reflects aspects of the French national temperament no less than the Italian Communists reflect the subtlety and quicksilver flexibility so characteristic of their countrymen at large.

By insisting that Communists, of whatever country or color, are all the same, Western states only succeed in driving them into each other's arms. Communists are all different. They were different in the days when, by insisting that Russia and China were indivisible, the Western world actively helped to keep those two countries together. They are very different now.

Moscow's Position

In Moscow's eyes, the only good foreign Communist is one who obeys the Kremlin's instructions without question, as in East Germany, in Bulgaria, and in Czechoslovakia since the 1968 invasion; in Poland, Hungary, or Rumania, Gierek, Kadar, and Ceausescu are all awkward customers in their very different ways. At the same time, Moscow is never really happy about the Communists of any country that is not adjacent to the Soviet Union—and thus not immediately accessible to Soviet tanks—or that is not permanently garrisoned by Soviet troops.

A successful show of independence on the part of any Communist party beyond the immediate reach of the Soviet army is something the Russians regard with apprehension, alarm and even fear, for its disruptive effect on their Eastern European satellites. Ever since 1948, Titoism has been regarded by the Russians as an open wound in the body of the Soviet bloc, inviting infection and corruption. And, of course, they have been right to see it so. Without the example of Yugoslavia, there would have been no attempt in Czechoslovakia, just twenty years later, to let in light and air. And we know that poor Dubček had to be put down with a public display of brute force that sickened the world—not only because the East Germans and other Soviet-bloc Communists were stricken by the fear that their own people might start to follow the Czechoslovak example, but also because the Russians feared that their own non-Russian peoples (most dangerously, the Ukrainians) might be similarly inspired.

From Moscow's standpoint, the first duty of a foreign Communist party is not to conduct experiments in revolution or succor the working class but to underwrite the security of the Soviet Union. And the Soviet Union, like Czarist Russia, is always uneasy with an independent ally and has no idea how to handle a dependent one with tact and flexibility. Leonid Brezhnev hauling some fraternal comrade over the coals for betraying the sacred cause of Lenin is reminiscent of Nicholas I reproaching his brother-in-law, King Frederick William IV of Prussia, for being soft toward the revolutionaries in 1848, bitterly accusing him of betraying his royal trust.

Issues in Independence

The Russians, of course, are right in a way. They can no longer believe in the victory of a world revolution effortlessly presided over by Moscow. (What would happen to

Moscow if America went Communist and started throwing
its weight about? There's a nightmare for the Kremlin!) So,
to the Russians, the Communist parties of Europe have only
one use—to keep the Western allies individually and collectively vulnerable to subversion, without going too far and
plunging the whole continent into chaos at a time when
Russia still requires help from the advanced economies.
Above all, the Russians need to use the foreign parties to
make Western governments feel the potential power of
communism. And Western governments, alas, all too often
play into the Russians' hand by exaggerating that power.

In order that they may use foreign parties for their own
ends, the Russians have to keep the strictest possible control
over their movements. Once this control is lost, anything
may happen. It seems to me that Eurocommunism has
already gone so far that Moscow has lost not merely control
but also understanding of where the European comrades are
going. I am also fairly sure that the European comrades
hardly know where they are going themselves. With the
exception of the Spanish party, and to a slightly less emphatic degree, the Italians, they are still, to all appearances,
tied to Moscow. But do they really believe in Moscow, or is
this bond no more than a habit of mind or, even, a matter of
expediency? And, in particular, are they so conditioned that
their first thought, if they should come to share secrets of
state, would be to pass on those secrets to the Kremlin?

The Tradition of Dissent

It is useful at this point to go back a little. . . . [In] summer [1977], the Spanish Communist Santiago Carrillo publicly declared that the Soviet Union could no longer be
regarded as a Socialist state (presumably he shared the view
of most non-Communists that the Russian system is only a
form of state capitalism). Although assailed sharply by Moscow, he was not disowned by any of the West European
parties and was treated sympathetically by Poland, Hungary,
and Yugoslavia. How did this become possible?

It all began with Khrushchev. In his public address (as

opposed to his secret speech) to the twentieth Soviet party congress in January 1956, he solemnly revised the Leninist canon. Lenin had insisted that there was only one way of making a true revolution in Russia—the Bolshevik way, his way; all others were vain imitations, and criminal into the bargain. In due course, the Bolshevik way, Lenin's way, hardened into a model for the world. At the same time, he categorically laid down the canon that world revolution could be achieved only through a series of major wars.

In Lenin's day, this sounded grand and apocalyptic, if one liked that sort of thing. But in the atomic age, it made no sense at all. Stalin, just before he died [in 1953] was cautiously starting to revise the canon in the light of the nuclear facts of life: there must be wars, he said, but the Soviet Union should be able to keep out of them. Malenkov, as soon as he took over, went much further and said that war in the atomic age was unthinkable. Khrushchev, for his own purposes, attacked Malenkov violently for this heresy. Yet as soon as Malenkov was down, Khrushchev appropriated the idea, as Stalin had appropriated some of Trotsky's ideas when that great demagogue was down.

Khrushchev's contribution at the 1956 party congress was that war was no longer "fatally inevitable." He went further—mostly to please Marshal Tito, to whom he had rather clumsily apologized the year before for Stalin's savage treatment of Yugoslavia in 1948. . . . Different countries, Khrushchev declared, might take different ways to socialism. And he went further still. There were those among the Western Communists who even then were privately airing doubts as to whether Russian- or even Balkan- or South American-style revolutions were applicable to the advanced industrial countries. . . . Khrushchev acknowledged that in certain lands and in certain circumstances, revolution might be achieved by peaceful means.

For the world at large, these pronouncements were soon overshadowed by the revelations of Khrushchev's secret speech, with its story of Stalin's crimes, but they were not forgotten by the European Communist parties. And before long those statements were being exploited in a manner not at all foreseen by Khrushchev himself.

Quite soon after the party congress, the veteran Italian Communist leader Palmiro Togliatti took Khrushchev to task for blaming all the evils that had befallen the Soviet Union on Stalin. . . . There must be something wrong with a system that had permitted a Stalin to flourish unopposed, and it was high time the Moscow comrades pulled themselves together and tried to improve that system very radically indeed. But that was only one voice.

The 1960 Congress: Attack from Both Sides

The first major occasion for a general airing of Western European Communist thinking on the subject was provided by the celebrated Moscow conference of eighty-one Communist parties in December 1960. Curiously enough, it was the Chinese who gave the Europeans the chance to tell the Russians with perfect impunity something of what they thought of them.

The conference will go down in history as a grand climacteric. It was the last time that almost all the Communist parties of the world got together, meeting in secret and presenting to the outside world a monolithic image. That image was about as far from the truth as it is possible to imagine. The great quarrel between Russia and China had started up in earnest nearly a year earlier, and had been revealed to a chosen few at a meeting in Bucharest the previous summer. Now delegates from all the parties were treated to the unnerving spectacle of Khrushchev and Teng Hsiao-ping shouting each other down like fishwives in the Great Hall of the Kremlin. At this stage, the outer world knew nothing of the quarrel or of Moscow's desperate need for support against Chinese pretensions.

What happened was that the Chinese attacked Khrushchev as the betrayer of Leninism not only for his condemnation of Stalin but especially for his reconciliation with Marshal Tito, his acceptance of different paths to socialism and his rejection of the "fatal inevitability" of war. All this, they insisted, was nothing less than "revisionism," the most deadly sin in Bolshevik eyes.

Revisionism, for all practical purposes, meant the concept of evolutionary (as opposed to revolutionary) socialism, as proposed at the turn of the century by the distinguished German Socialist Eduard Bernstein, who was consigned to outer darkness by Lenin for holding that society might be transformed, capitalism abolished and socialism enthroned by peaceful means. Now, in Moscow, in the winter of 1960, a very paradoxical situation arose. The Chinese were quite correct in accusing Khrushchev of revisionism, but the Europeans, in coming to his support and accusing Peking of obscurantism, were able to compound that very sin and thus push the case for their own independence much further than the Russians liked. . . .

Most . . . [Europeans] had been critical of Moscow ever since the 1956 Hungarian uprising; and . . . [now were] deeply upset by the crudely high-handed manner in which their Soviet hosts had tried to stage-manage the whole affair, briefing the visitors in an obviously equivocal and tendentious way and, worse, treating the various delegations almost like prisoners under house arrest, and keeping them rigidly apart so that it was impossible for them to meet and compare notes.

Now they had their chance, and they took it. The Russians could do nothing to curb them without appearing to take China's side. Thus, they had to sit and listen in their own Moscow stronghold to the Swedish party secretary, Hilding Hagberg, declaring that there was no sense in parroting Lenin without taking note of the changes since his time. Furthermore, the Swedish as well as the Swiss comrades announced that they found all talk about the dictatorship of the proletariat (still a sacred and unquestioned phrase) anachronistic and distasteful. Even Maurice Thorez of France, hitherto grimly loyal to Moscow, if only because of his hatred of the Italians, agreed with this.

Luigi Longo, the Italian representative, continued the Togliatti line with considerable panache, blazing the reformist and revisionist trail under cover of support for Moscow against the Chinese heresy hunters. But it was the Swede, once again, who declared less equivocally than any of his colleagues that the hatchet must be buried between the Communists and their most hated opponents, hated far more than any right-wing party—the Social Democrats. The Swedish Communist party, he said, had decided to give up fighting the ruling Social Democrats once and for all. They were now working for the day when the two parties would be fused into one.

Here the Swedish party was on the most treacherous ground imaginable. For Soviet communism as we know it today arose from Lenin's bitter quarrel with some of his closest colleagues—fellow members of the Russian Social Democratic Labor party, which he split irrevocably into two wings, Bolshevik and Menshevik. . . . Ever since Lenin's day, Social Democrats all over the world have been anathematized by the Communists and pursued with the unrelenting hatred reserved for heretics.

Now in 1960, forty-one years after the foundation of the Third International, reunion with the heretics was being proposed all over again, this time by the Communist Party of Sweden, with the seeming approval of the other Western European Communist delegates.

As I have said, the outside world knew nothing at the time of what went on at that Moscow conference, which was presented as a show of solidarity and force and was accepted as such by most outsiders. A few months later, I was able to reveal in some detail the story of the Sino-Soviet quarrel, but it was not until 1963 that a number of the other Communist parties, most notably the Italian, French and Belgian, began to publish in their journals accounts of their own contributions.

New Efforts at Control

The following year, Khrushchev was overthrown, and Communist affairs stagnated while his successors sorted themselves out, attended to urgent domestic matters and found their bearings. But in 1968, when the Russians re-acted with such characteristic brutality to the Czechoslovak party's attempt to civilize itself, the Western European par-ties for the first time came out in open and public condem-nation of Moscow's action. . . .

Since 1968, one of Brezhnev's main preoccupations has been to bring those Europeans under stricter control. He has failed. One measure of his failure was their stubborn resistance to an idea behind which he was putting all his weight—a conference of European parties to affirm and for-malize total unity, a unity presided over by the Communist party of the Soviet Union.

The European Communists resisted, first, to the holding of a conference at all; then, when the meeting was held in 1976, to Soviet attempts to rig it in Moscow's favor; and after that to Moscow's renewed attempts, despite a rebuff at the conference, to reassert Soviet hegemony over the whole Communist world and excommunicate China. And it was during the organization of this resistance that the term Eurocommunism began to come into use. [For details on these efforts see Daniel Seligman's "A Crisis of Authority," above in Section I.—Ed.]

Carrillo Versus Moscow and the Limits of Independence

A still more striking measure of Brezhnev's failure has been Carrillo's scathing criticism and the way in which the West European comrades rallied to his support when Mos-cow opened up on him with its big guns, including a blast from the Soviet foreign-policy weekly *New Times*. Indeed, they forced the Russians to withdraw. In a second article, *New Times* declared that it was all a misunderstanding arising from slanders in the bourgeois press; that Moscow had nothing against the respected Spanish party, only against Carrillo personally. This line was promptly de-nounced by the French as an impermissible attempt by Moscow to make trouble between a fraternal party and its chosen leader. And there the matter rests—but not, I think, for long.

What does all this amount to? As we all know, the lie is a most favored weapon in the Communist armory, and the techniques of deception and softening up are highly developed. It has also to be remembered that the Communist parties of Western Europe contain some extremely tough individuals. The men who are now speaking out against some of Moscow's policies and attitudes include some who, for a very long time, accepted Stalin as their master, holding him up to the rest of the world as a great and benevolent leader and pursuing anyone who tried to tell the truth about his crimes (e.g., the present writer) with a sustained venom hard for anyone who has not been the object of it to imagine.

Even more interestingly, in spite of Stalin, in spite of Hungary, in spite of Prague, in spite of Brezhnev's continuing persecution of so many brave and distinguished men and women who ask only for the chance to help the Soviet system approximate more closely the ideals it professes (to say nothing of the Jews), in spite of the sadly obvious fact that in Poland, Hungary, East Germany, Czechoslovakia and even Rumania, Soviet rule means domination of the more advanced by the more backward—in spite of all this and more besides, Carrillo is so far the only Eurocommunist leader to pronounce the simple truth well known to all the fraternal comrades—namely, that the Soviet Union cannot be called a Socialist country—and to take the logical next step—namely, to urge the Eurocommunists to set themselves up against Moscow as the champions of real socialism. Italy's Berlinguer, in a speech before his party's Central Committee . . . [in January 1978], seemed to have implied the same message, but his words were ambiguous. All the others, however sharply they may criticize some of the Kremlin's activities, preserve their links with Moscow as the acknowledged headquarters of the world Communist movement.

Why? Is it because, in spite of their reservations about the Russian way of doing things, they are still working for the Kremlin, as they most certainly did in the past? Do they dream of the day when, by whatever means, they win power in their own countries and will then proudly announce to whoever is then sitting at the top of the pile in the Kremlin: "Sire! Italy [or France, or Luxembourg] is at your feet!" And the Brezhnev of the day will then smile and say, "Well done, good and faithful servant! Go thou and rule in my name in just the way you think best." Will they then show themselves as being aliens in their own countries and among their own people—become Russian puppets, like Ulbricht in Germany, Gottwald in Czechoslovakia, Rakosi in Hungary, and the rest?

A Tenuous Solidarity

That seems improbable to me. It seems far more likely that the present links with Moscow, varying in strength from party to party, are being maintained partly for what can be gotten from the Soviet Union in the way of material and moral support but far more from habit, for the sake of a feeling of solidarity with some sort of world movement, even if the chairman is not all that might be desired. When all is said, they have come very close to endorsing Carrillo's most extreme statements by the very act of not condemning them as outrageous and criminal.

And a further sign of the times may be found in the reaction of some of the Soviet-bloc parties to the first New Times article. The Czechs, as would be expected from a government installed by Marshal Grechko after the destruction of "socialism with a human face," were abusive to the point of hysteria in their condemnation of the Spaniards, But the Poles managed to get by without saying anything at all, simply publishing the New Times article rather belatedly and without comment. While the Hungarians, following Kadar's familiar line, expressed continued sympathy with Eurocommunism, upheld the idea of different paths to socialism, and only very gently urged good Communists to refrain from questioning the "victorious path" taken by other Socialist countries in the past.

Motives for Autonomy: More Than Opportunism

It is important to remember two things. The first is that the original bosses of the Eastern European parties were nothing but Stalin's puppets, installed and protected by the Soviet Army, without which they would never have attained power. The one Communist head of state who fought his own way to power and had next to no help from Moscow—Marshal Tito—soon made it clear that he proposed to remain his own master. Should we expect Western European Communists, who have also had to make their own way, to forget their nationality any more than Tito? Or to subdue their very much more advanced economies and cultures to the backward, unattractive, uncomprehending parvenus in the Kremlin?

The second thing to remember is the nature of the Communist voters in the Western European countries. In Britain, these tend to be fanatical, but they are pathetically few. In Italy and France, they are counted in millions, and they include some fanatics, of course, but the vast majority are not Communists at all, in the sense of being disciplined ideologues: They are radical protesters, very much French and Italians first, but disillusioned with the older parties. It is inconceivable to me that, even if he so wished, a Marchais in France or a Berlinguer in Italy could carry his countrymen into the Soviet camp and hand them over to Brezhnev, or whomever, without provoking a civil war.

And it is no answer to retort that the Italians and the Germans between the wars had no difficulty in delivering themselves into slavery at the hands of Mussolini and Hitler. The appeal of both these creatures, in their very different ways, was precisely to the spirit of nationalism—chauvinistic and unashamed. Carrillo declared that if Moscow had attacked him sooner, it would have been worth many more votes to him at the recent Spanish election, and this is the sort of factor that Communist leaders in other lands must bear in mind.

It could be argued that the Eurocommunists are exhibiting measured antagonism to Moscow and appealing to reason and common sense simply to deceive and attract more voters to their side. Even if that were so, and they win those additional voters, will it make them, in the long run, any stronger? I think not. I think that the very existence of Eurocommunism has weakened the Soviet position irretrievably. Further, that a point will soon be reached at which the success and growing influence of the Communist parties, and their involvement with the established parties, will turn the scales against them. Rather than frightening away their moderately inclined supporters, they will have disgusted their more radical supporters and driven them into splinter groups, to Maoism or Trotskyism—anything but Brezhnevism, which is Russian imperialism writ very large and in red letters, and of use to self-respecting revolutionaries only insofar as it can be persuaded to back them with arms or hard cash.

The Russians may not understand all this, but I think they have grasped the central fact—the weakening of their own power by the reduction of their fifth-column influence in Western Europe. The decline of Soviet communism does not, by any means, imply the decline of revolutionary activities in the West. Far from it. And one of the questions it is necessary to ask is whether we are not allowing ourselves to be dangerously diverted by thinking too much about Eurocommunism and not enough about the various militant extremists—terrorists of various colors, anarchists, so-called Maoists and Trotskyites—whose activities are already too familiar and who are dedicated to the overthrow of the established order.

Authoritarianism: A Universal Issue

There is, of course, another question to be asked about the Eurocommunists. If they attain power—even in ideological opposition to Soviet communism—what sort of government are they likely to provide? Can the freedoms West Europeans now enjoy hope to survive?

There is no straight answer. Berlinguer of Italy has said that his party, if it came to power, would tolerate opposition parties, and, furthermore, would be prepared to hold elections and to surrender office if voted out. There is no way of knowing how true this is. My own view is that, just as the Soviet Communist party was colored, conditioned and shaped by the character of the backward, cunning, ignorant, suspicious peasants who came to dominate it once the revolution had succeeded, so communism in Italy and France has already been colored and shaped by the character of the people of those countries, who would go on behaving very much as in the past. I believe that unless the Communist parties can rally the Italians and the French with patriotic war cries, they will fail. I believe that a resurgence of some sort of right-wing extremism is more likely than the victory of Moscow-led communism. This means that European communism must either go on transforming itself, or fall apart.

It seems to me fairly obvious that with any sort of Communist party in power in any country, there would be a great deal more authoritarianism than exists at present in the Western democracies, which vary among themselves on that score. But this problem of the authoritarian state transcends the problem of communism. If the Soviet Union were swallowed up tomorrow, we would still be faced with the problem of how a world of rapidly increasing populations dependent on relatively dwindling resources can be organized and held together without resort to totalitarian methods, moderate or extreme, left or right. One of the most unfortunate consequences of Lenin, it seems to me, is that the bogy of Russian communism has effectively prevented us from thinking straight about this very urgent problem.

In other words, the growth of Eurocommunism, and its appeal, owes far, far more to the failures of the Western world than to Moscow. I mean, for example, our failure to deal adequately with such continuing scandals as excessive unemployment, and the failure of people who pass for leaders of our societies to find a language to share with the idealistic young, who in frustration turn, at best, to cynicism and apathy; at worst, to violence.

FROM WEST TO EAST:
A REVERSAL OF INFLUENCE?[2]

During the almost six decades that have passed since the
Russian Revolution of 1917, two contradictory qualities
have distinguished the international Communist movement.
One has been the persistent Soviet effort to subordinate
the interests of foreign Communist parties to those of the
Communist party of the Soviet Union (CPSU); the other
has been the equally persistent effort of these parties to resist such "Sovietization" and, in the process, to question
Moscow's leading role in world communism. Now, in the
aftermath of . . . [the summer 1976] Conference of European Communist Parties in Berlin, a third tendency may
be observed in the international relations of the Communist
movement—the prospective export of what has come to be
known as "Eurocommunism" *from West to East*, signifying
a historic shift in the direction of influence and initiative
within world communism.

At issue, then, is no longer only the much-discussed
challenge to the primacy of Russian interests in the Communist movement. After all, most foreign Communists have
long refused to see themselves as instruments of Soviet
foreign policy or, more generally, to allow Moscow to impose its will on them. Tito's Yugoslavia defied the Soviet
Union as early as 1948–1949; the Italian Communist party
(PCI), under Palmiro Togliatti, advanced the once unthinkable notion of polycentrism soon after Stalin's death in
1953; and China's opposition to the leading role of the
CPSU began to surface only a few years thereafter. Indeed,
the classic Soviet definition of a Communist revolutionary
—as one who "without evasions, unconditionally, openly,
and honestly" makes the cause of world revolution synonymous with the interests and, indeed, with the defense of the

[2] Article entitled "The 'Europeanization' of Communism?" by Charles Gati,
chairman of the department of political science at Union College, coauthor of
The Debate Over Détente and other works on politics and communism. *Foreign Affairs.* 55:539-53. Ap. '77. Reprinted by permission from *Foreign
Affairs*, April 1977. Copyright 1977 by Council on Foreign Relations, Inc.

USSR—has long become an embarrassing reminder of a past most Communist parties in the world would rather forget.

West and East European "Autonomism"

What we are beginning to witness now is the active promotion by the more moderate European parties of their own brand of socialism. In their search for popular support and respectability—and perhaps guided by considerations of principle as well—the "Eurocommunists" of Italy, Spain, and, to a lesser extent, France have come to present their vision of "socialism with liberty" as one with both West and East European, if not quite universal, applicability. Having gone beyond criticism of single events in the East— such as the Soviet-led invasion of Czechoslovakia or the harassment of dissenters in several of the ruling party-states —they now press for the emulation of their own concepts and, hence, for systemic political change in Eastern Europe and eventually the Soviet Union itself.

Professor Lucio Lombardo Radice, a leading member of the PCI's Central Committee, for example, recently expressed the view that it was "inevitable that the Italian, French, or Spanish 'model' should become a political problem for the ruling Communist parties." Linking Eurocommunism with the "Socialist opposition" in the East—he mentioned Medvedev in the Soviet Union and Havemann in the German Democratic Republic—Radice further argued that "one can no longer conceive of Eurocommunism as the regional variant of a strategy ordained by the official Marxism of the Socialist countries. The truth is that there is a clash between two general perspectives. What is at stake is the relationship between socialism and liberty, and the way that relationship is worked out is equally relevant to the Socialist and capitalist countries." ("Problemi dall'Est per il PCI: Il caso Biermann," *La Stampa* [Turin], December 8, 1976. In an early, pre-Berlin comment on Eurocommunism as an all-European phenomenon, Robert Kleiman observed that "democratic Communism in Italy and other West European countries might split the Communist world more profoundly than Titoism and undermine authoritarianism in East Europe." "Italy's Communist Tide," New York *Times,* December 2, 1975.)

That Eurocommunism is neither a "regional variant" of Communist doctrine nor a "political problem" for Western Europe alone was evidenced by the [1976] Berlin Conference of European Communist Parties. Countering Moscow's "official Marxism" and, indeed, dominating the conference were the "autonomist" parties of both Western and Eastern Europe—of France, Italy, Spain, Yugoslavia, Rumania and others. Even though the West European parties' proclaimed commitment to pluralism was notably absent from the stated positions or present practices of the East European parties of Yugoslavia and Rumania, what united them was their shared desire to resist Soviet ideological hegemony. With the Soviet leaders on the defensive, then, the proceedings vividly displayed the strength of the increasingly assertive Eurocommunist parties.

Three Central Questions

One measure of that strength and thus of the magnetism of the Eurocommunist phenomenon is the extent to which Eurocommunism poses an alternative to the more authoritarian Soviet model in world communism, particularly in Eastern Europe. To assess the prospects for such an eventuality, three questions must be raised: (1) Can the Eurocommunist objectives—including the gradual liberation of Soviet-style communism from its rigid and Byzantine features—be regarded as genuine? (2) Can Eurocommunism be exported to Eastern Europe—is it "transferable"? (3) Can the Soviet Union be expected to adjust itself to, or indeed to tolerate, the de-Russification and, hence, the Europeanization of communism?

Eurocommunism:
Autonomy, Pluralism and a Popular Front

Despite its apparent imprecision, the term *Eurocommunism* has gained wide currency as a convenient designation for a more tolerant, moderate, and democratic tendency in world communism. It refers, in particular, to the outlook of the Italian Communist party, with its long history of theoretical divergence and partial independence from Moscow under the leadership of [Antonio] Gramsci, Togliatti, and Berlinguer; but the term also connotes the outlook of other West European parties—notably those of Spain and France—which have only lately come to adopt some of the features of the Italians' ideological platform and political approach.

Underpinning that ideological platform are three interrelated propositions.

☐ First is the persistent demand by Eurocommunists that each party be free to apply the teachings of Marxism-Leninism according to national needs and circumstances. What is being advocated as "socialism in French colors" or "socialism Italian style" is, of course, tantamount to a rejection of the universal validity of the Soviet "model" or experience.

☐ Second is the Eurocommunists' disavowal of any claim to a monopoly of power and thus to the establishment of a "dictatorship of the proletariat." Declaring its respect for the "verdict of universal suffrage" and pledging its commitment to "freedom of opinion, of expression, of association, of the press, the right to strike, free movement of the people, et cetera," the program of the French Communist Party (PCF), for example, puts great emphasis on pluralism and "the uninterrupted extension of democracy."

☐ Third is the Eurocommunists' related interest in, and, indeed, their insistence upon the creation of a broad coalition of political forces to seek the resolution of pressing economic and social problems. Called the popular front or united front policy in the 1930s and 1940s—when it was widely regarded as a short-term tactical device to gain power—it proposes the cooperation of diverse political elements, some Marxist and some not, but all sharing a common program aimed at the reduction and, eventually, the elimination of the power of monopoly capital.

A Sense of Déjà Vu?

Perhaps the only novel formulation here is the Italian modification of the popular front policy through the advocacy of the "historic compromise." Instead of seeking a presumably narrow and very possibly shaky majority based exclusively on an alliance of the Left, the PCI has lately embraced the idea of a "grand coalition" that would include the centrist Christian Democrats as well. Responding to the lessons of Chile—in particular, to the military coup that overthrew President Allende's Popular Unity Front government of the Left in 1973 [see James Burnham's "Chile: A Study in Counterrevolution," in Section III, above]—the PCI has since sought to avoid a similar polarization of political forces in Italy, assuming that even if a Leftist coalition were to obtain a majority of the votes in a general election, it could not govern effectively if threatened by the prospect of civil strife. Accordingly, the party's 1976 election program stressed that "a possibility is emerging that never before existed in Italy and has few parallels in other countries: the possibility of collaboration among various forces which, without abandoning their own ideologies, . . . [can] work for common political and social goals in the common interest." In short, the PCI regards the "historic compromise" not only as the only viable political alternative to economic stagnation and chaos, but as a major step toward the once-heretical idea of accommodation between the country's working classes on the one hand and the middle class on the other.

Whether the "historic compromise" is merely a skillful variation on the popular front theme under changing conditions or whether it actually represents the repudiation of popular front policies remains an open question. The rest of the Eurocommunist platform, however, is more likely to invoke both a sense of skepticism and a feeling of déjà vu in Western students of Communist politics.

For one thing, the Eurocommunist positions strikingly resemble those advanced by *East* European party leaders after World War II—just prior to their seizure of power.

After all, it was not Enrico Berlinguer in 1977 but the Stalinist Jozsef Revai of the Hungarian party in 1944 who said, "I declare that we do not regard the national collaboration [of the several parties] as a passing, political coalition, as a tactical chess move, but rather as a long-lasting alliance. We will stand by our given word." In a similar vein, it was the Bulgarian Georgi Dimitrov, one-time General Secretary of the Communist International, who stated at the November 7, 1945, anniversary celebration of the Russian Revolution in Moscow that the "assertion that the Communists allegedly want to seize full power . . . is a malicious legend and slander. It is not true that the Communists want to have a single party government." And it was Wladyslaw Gomulka of the Polish Party who declared in 1946 that the Polish road to socialism is "significant because it does not include the necessity of a violent, revolutionary, political upheaval . . . [it has] eliminated the necessity of a dictatorship of the proletariat."

The West European party leaders' own statements should also generate some doubts about their long-term commitment to the democratic process. In a secret speech to the Central Committee of the [French] PCF in June 1972—the contents of which were disclosed three years later—Georges Marchais had referred to the Communist-Socialist union of the Left as one "favoring intervention of the masses, a springboard for the people's movement and for the development of its action." By using such code words, he seemed to suggest that the Communist concessions implicit in the joint platform of the Left were more apparent than real, and that they would pave the way to the realization of the party's essentially unchanged objectives. In another speech, Marchais explained what the PCF had apparently meant by a multiparty system. Although no one familiar with what is left of the once predominant Polish Peasant party or with East Germany's dormant Christian Democratic Union would ever mistake them for active partners in a genuine multiparty system, Marchais, alluding to the ruling Communist party-states, claimed that "of the fourteen Socialist countries, a single party exists in only six, while there are two or more parties in the other eight."

A Different Situation

Nevertheless, the main issue is neither the sincerity of the Eurocommunists' professed intentions nor the similarity between their statements and those of the East European parties in the postwar years. Historical analogies can be—and in this case probably are—quite misleading, for the very special circumstances that existed in Eastern Europe after World War II simply do not pertain to Western Europe in the 1970s. To begin with the most obvious factor, the political allegiance of Eastern Europe was ultimately determined by the proximity of the Soviet Union and the presence of the Red army. In addition—contrary to revisionist interpretations of recent vintage—the West could provide no more than verbal encouragement to indigenous non-Communist elements during their struggle for power. The profound social, economic and political crisis that followed in the wake of the war's devastation and the collapse of the region's old regimes also created circumstances calling for *some* radical remedy. Finally, with the notable exception of Czechoslovakia, the imposition of authoritarian rule was abetted throughout Eastern Europe by the absence of adequate training and experience in political democracy.

By contrast, while prevailing internal conditions in some of the West European countries may well make Communist participation in a governing coalition possible and perhaps even necessary, international conditions would seem to impede the fulfillment of any residual Communist ambitions for hegemony. Aside from obvious geopolitical factors—which make the Soviet Union a distant, albeit interested, observer—economic interdependence within the Common Market combined with extensive commercial ties between the United States and individual West European countries tend to militate against the establishment of a one-party Communist state. Even the experience of Portugal—a country largely outside the mainstream of West European economic life—suggests that external pressure through economic leverage, such as the withholding of aid, can translate into considerable political influence.

Nor should one underestimate the continuing political strength of indigenous democratic forces in Western Europe. In view of the still vigorous, if cautious, backing of Italy's Christian Democrats by the Catholic church, it is surely premature to dismiss their popular appeal. In France, where both the Communist-Socialist alliance and the Gaullist coalition are embroiled in contentious maneuverings, the polls suggest dramatic gains in popular support for François Mitterrand's Socialist party and a slight, but significant, decline for the PCF. While Mitterrand remains strongly opposed to a centrist coalition with President Giscard d'Estaing—and thus to the isolation of Jacques Chirac's Gaullist movement on the Right and the Communists on the Left—the Socialists' impressive comeback to a position of senior status within the Left alliance and their strained relationship with the PCF do combine to create a new opportunity for a non-Communist political alternative.

Democratic Precedents of Communist Parties

There is something to be said for the record of the West European Communist parties as well. At one time or another since World War II, particularly between 1945 and 1947, Communists joined the governments of France, Italy, Belgium, Luxembourg, Austria, Greece, Norway, Denmark, Iceland and Finland; they helped keep the Swedish Social Democrats in power for years as they now assist the Christian Democratic party of Italy; and they managed, or participated in the management of, municipal governments in hundreds of cities and towns throughout Western Europe. Indeed, part of their present appeal stems from a record of efficiency and integrity in local governing bodies. More important, only in Greece—under chaotic political conditions three decades ago—did one of these Communist parties make an overt move toward political hegemony. That the others did not do so does not mean, of course, that they either did not wish to or that they might not do so in the future; rather it means that in the face of counter-vailing power—be that the strength of domestic political competitors or the fear of external reaction—they have quite consistently opted for a cautious course and, indeed, for what seemed politically feasible under the circumstances.

All in all, the Eurocommunist parties' past experience in office, their opponents' political skill and enduring appeal and, above all, the international environment within which they operate constitute the main conditions circumscribing their strategy. Convinced of the soundness of their goals, they have kept that strategy highly competitive and asser-tive. Quite naturally, they seek more power and influence. The question, however, is not so much what their final goals may be but whether they are sufficiently restrained to seek only what is attainable even if it conflicts with what they consider ultimately desirable. Paradoxically, then, one can remain skeptical about their long-term commitment to political pluralism and still concede the authenticity of their limited objectives; for, given prevailing conditions now and in the foreseeable future, as well as the lessons of Chile and Portugal, the only way for the Eurocommunists to ease into positions of power is to forestall the kind of in-ternal and external reaction that would only blunt their apparent momentum.

If electoral necessity indicates a cautious strategy and a responsible posture at home, it requires a foreign policy platform that not only dissociates Eurocommunism from the oppressive qualities of Soviet-style authoritarian rule but also insists upon the expansion of individual liberty and national autonomy in the East. For in an atmosphere of lingering suspicions, the West European Communist parties continue to suffer from what the East European Communist parties do or fail to do and, indeed, from the very imposition of Soviet power on Eastern Europe.

For East Europeans, on the other hand, Eurocommunism

is a promising source of ideological justification and political leverage in their search for more independence from Moscow. It tends to reinforce the image East Europeans have always had of their historic role in Europe as a bridge between East and West and, more recently, as a kind of ideological potting shed for the introduction of Western ideas into the Soviet Union. In addition, Eurocommunism falls on fertile soil in Eastern Europe; after all, its early variant—national communism—was born in Yugoslavia and then nurtured, though not always successfully, by Imre Nagy in Hungary, Wladyslaw Gomulka in Poland, Alexander Dubček in Czechoslovakia, Gheorghe Gheorghiu-Dej and Nicolae Ceausescu in Rumania, and others.

But the East European elites' attraction to Eurocommunism derives mainly from their traditional belief in the impact of international developments on the processes of internal change and their reliance on it in charting their political strategies. The past shows that they have used and even manipulated various international alignments and trends to serve domestic political ends. De-Stalinization in the mid-1950s, the Sino-Soviet rift in the early 1960s, the presumed uncertainty of the new Brezhnev regime in the mid-1960s, and such Western manifestations as the promises of *Ostpolitik* [West Germany's Eastern policy] and of the Soviet-American détente during the last decade have all been utilized—individually and collectively, directly and indirectly—to help modify the political profile of Eastern Europe. That the otherwise highly authoritarian Albanian regime could escape Soviet domination and Rumanian foreign policy could diverge from Moscow's international positions was, of course, facilitated by the Sino-Soviet rift. That the Hungarians' New Economic Mechanism and the ill-fated Czechoslovak experiment in "socialism with a human face" could gain ground was due to the initial sense of uncertainty the post-Khrushchev leadership had projected between 1964 and 1968.

Today, East Europeans widely predict and earnestly anticipate the effect of Eurocommunism on their region. Because it is sponsored by Communist parties with which the Soviet Union maintains a comradely, if guarded, relationship, and because it has acquired considerable legitimacy in world communism, Eurocommunism is viewed as a viable within-system alternative to the Soviet model. In fact, as an alternative to prevailing theory and practice, it may prove to be the most potent foreign stimulus to have affected Eastern Europe since the convulsion produced by de-Stalinization in the mid-1950s.

Like de-Stalinization, Eurocommunism also confronts Eastern Europe with the almost certain prospect of further atomization. Significant differences have already surfaced between those who welcome the political opportunity inherent in Eurocommunism and those who fear its consequences. As of now, the "autonomist" parties of Yugoslavia, Rumania and Albania are actively promoting and anxiously protecting their own brand of socialism, while Yugoslavia has already adopted not only many of the foreign policy features but also some of the domestic planks of the Eurocommunist platform. At the other end of the political spectrum, the "loyalist" parties of Bulgaria, Czechoslovakia and East Germany remain deeply suspicious of Eurocommunist declarations of independence from Moscow, even though intellectuals in both Czechoslovakia and East Germany have recently invoked Eurocommunism to legitimize their demands for cultural freedom. Finally, the rather ambiguous Polish and Hungarian appraisals of the Eurocommunist phenomenon suggest internal debates in these two "centrist" parties between loyalist leaders who maintain that closer identification with Eurocommunism could jeopardize their delicate relationship with the Soviet Union, and autonomist leaders who claim that rejection of all aspects of Eurocommunism could upset the precarious balance at home.

Internal Conditions

Like other external stimuli in the past, then, Eurocom-munism has galvanized a new and divisive debate through-out Eastern Europe, impelling a timely reassessment of po-litical options. The result of these deliberations remains an open question. It seems clear, however, that the ulti-mate response of the East European regimes to Eurocom-munism is going to depend less on the loyalists' ideological reservations than on the adjustments these regimes believe they must make under changing social, economic and po-litical conditions.

Of these conditions, the potentially most explosive now is the assertive mood of the industrial working class. Last summer's [1976] violent food riots and strikes in Poland in-dicate not only the workers' dissatisfaction with economic conditions but also their willingness to take considerable risks to advance their interests. That the Polish government would immediately cancel the proposed price increases and then punish the workers less severely than their intellectual defenders also suggests that a Communist regime cannot easily resort to repressive measures against its own working class. It is one thing to silence or even imprison critical intellectuals; it is something else to stifle workers on whose behalf all Communist parties claim to govern.

Although such large-scale riots and strikes have not oc-curred elsewhere, there is apprehension everywhere in Eastern Europe about the implications of the Polish events. [See "Eastern Europe: Consumer Unrest and Concessions," by D. A. Andelman, in Section I, above.] For, in addition to facing the persistent economic dilemma of how to combine economic growth with an improved standard of living, the Communist party-states are also confronted with the equally persistent political dilemma of how to avoid similar outbreaks by providing orderly procedures for the expression of legitimate grievances. (Aside from Yugo-slavia, so far only the Hungarian party has sought to use the otherwise timid and party-controlled trade unions as a forum for the articulation of working-class interests, but in this case the unions' rather narrow-minded leaders have used them less *for* the industrial working class than *against* the increasingly prosperous peasantry and the technical-managerial-professional middle class.)

Inherent in the active manifestation of working-class discontent, moreover, is the failure of the East European regimes to reconcile the needs of rather sophisticated economic systems with the professed ideological imperative of centralized political control. Their inability to make the necessary systemic adjustments is reflected in the ongoing confrontation within the elites between reformist modernizers—who promote decentralization, material incentives, and reliance on nonparty expertise—and the more purist members of the party elites who consider such measures contrary to proper ideological standards. The issue is whether new impetus can be given to the region's deficient economic systems solely within the confines of prevailing ideological and political limitations, or whether—given the impact of global inflation, growing foreign indebtedness, inadequate technological innovation, low productivity, and, in some countries, severe shortages of food and consumer products—fresh political initiatives and ideological flexibility have become unavoidable. In their search for the good society, then, the proprietors of power in Eastern Europe must choose between relying on purely economic palliatives or acquiescing in incremental political concessions.

Common Dilemmas; Eurocommunist Solutions

This is where Eurocommunism intersects with the dilemmas of Eastern Europe. For, under admittedly different circumstances, the Eurocommunists have come to recognize that the restructuring of the economic base necessitates far-reaching reform of both their own political concepts and of the political system as a whole. While the PCI platform, for example, speaks of economic measures to curtail inflation, increase productivity, and develop more sophisticated technology, and while the PCF has addressed itself to the issue of excessive foreign debts and the dangers of a highly centralized economy as well, it is clear that, in the Eurocommunists' view, only their participation in political change can solve the "general crisis of capitalism" in Western Europe. Advocating greater political access, involvement and participation in the political process, the West European Communists affirm not the intrinsic merits of a pluralistic polity, but the liberating contribution to economic efficiency of broadly based, more open and inclusive political systems.

Should the party-states of Eastern Europe realize that the only way to economic salvation is through the gradual opening-up of *their* political process, they would find in the selective adoption of the Eurocommunist platform a convenient, if potentially destabilizing, guide to action. Assuming that they would tinker with the present political system only as much as they believed necessary and assuming, further, that they would proceed with circumspection, they might emulate the intriguing and admittedly tenuous formula the Italian Christian Democrats have recently worked out with the PCI. The Italian formula is a peculiar variant of political cooperation: PCI consultation and assistance combined with the Christian Democrats' retaining ultimate responsibility for the exercise of political power. [For further discussion see "Europe's Reds: Troubles for Moscow," by Edward Crankshaw, in this section, above.] Adapted to conditions now prevalent in Eastern Europe, the Communist parties would continue to control the major levers of power, but they would seek to coopt such political elements as they must, with the industrial working class involved in the management of factories—for which the moderately successful Yugoslav "workers' councils" might serve as a model—and the intelligentsia participating in the formulation of cultural and economic policies. Eastern Europe could also revive its venerable tradition of parliamentary activity (which even in the past only seldom coincided with Western-style competitive party systems), by allowing contested elections between two or more candidates of similar orientation vying for a seat, and by encouraging genuine legislative debates about public policy, including budgetary priorities. Even these limited reforms would begin to provide for a modicum of historical continuity, convey a commitment to a more open society and, in the end, contribute to the legitimacy of the regimes.

Such a Eurocommunist Eastern Europe would likely mitigate persistent socioeconomic problems and, in particular, allay working class discontent by infusing the East European publics with a sense of political rejuvenation. Furthermore, by promoting, however cautiously, the twin goals of political liberty, and national autonomy, a Eurocommunist Eastern Europe would apply itself to the vital tasks of appeasing intellectual dissenters and, most important, satisfying presently unfulfilled national aspirations.

A Soviet Backlash?

The Eurocommunist antimodel is thus a profound challenge to Soviet theory and practice; even its partial introduction into Eastern Europe might serve to unite the Soviet leadership behind a rigid, conservative and possibly violent reaction.

To the extent that its security depends on Eastern Europe, the Soviet Union would fear the gradual disintegration of the Warsaw Pact. To the extent that its economy depends on extensive trade with Eastern Europe—particularly with East Germany, Czechoslovakia and Poland—the Soviet Union would fear the weakening of bilateral economic ties and the fading away of the Council for Mutual Economic Assistance (COMECON). To the extent that the Soviet leaders insist on ideological primacy in Eastern Europe, they would fear being deprived of what is left of their universalist pretensions. To the extent, finally, that Moscow would accede to the legitimacy of a Eurocommunist Eastern Europe, it would fear domestic pressures for similar reforms in the Soviet Union itself.

While these fears may not always seem justified or compelling, on all too many occasions during the last three

decades—under Stalin, Khrushchev and Brezhnev—they have
served to spark harsh Soviet actions against threatening developments in Eastern Europe. Stalin's campaign may have
failed to reverse Yugoslavia's "revisionist" course, but his
brutal purges did contain—during his lifetime at least—
Tito's radiating influence elsewhere in Eastern Europe.
Prompted by such fears, Khrushchev crushed the Hungarian revolution in 1956 and Brezhnev did likewise with respect to the 1968 "Prague Spring." Even now, in this era
of peaceful coexistence, Moscow remains as firmly opposed
as ever to competing Socialist alternatives in the pro-Soviet
party-states of Eastern Europe, irrespective of whether they
are inspired by West European social democracy, Yugoslav
revisionism or, for that matter, Chinese "dogmatism."

Against this background, an uncompromising Soviet response to the introduction of Eurocommunist ideas into
Eastern Europe might well seem foreordained. After all, the
Soviet Union could not accept the Socialist program of
Dubček's "Eurocommunist" course in Czechoslovakia even
though, with the Communist party in a leading position, the
Dubček regime continued to operate on the basis of the one-
party system. In the end, Soviet intervention put an end to
the *limited* expansion of civil liberties, including freedom
of the press and assembly, curtailed popular participation
in the political process, and aborted the country's moderate
economic reforms.

Yet it is equally instructive to recall that, for several
months prior to their intervention, the Soviet leaders had
engaged in an almost desperate search for a nonmilitary
solution to the crisis. They had met the Czech leadership at
an unparalleled Politburo-to-Politburo summit as they
sought to persuade Dubček and his colleagues to slow down
the momentum, if not necessarily reverse the orientation, of
Prague's reformist course. They had also held extensive consultations with their East European allies, and it was the
East German Walter Ulbricht rather than Brezhnev who
most stubbornly advocated military action. (For a unique
eyewitness account of the July 1968 preinvasion summit of

Soviet and East European leaders in Warsaw, see Erwin Weit, *At the Red Summit: Interpreter Behind the Iron Curtain*, Macmillan, 1973, especially Chapter 11. Weit had been Gomulka's interpreter before defecting to the West.) Indeed, only after it became clear that the Dubček regime could neither mollify nor control ever-increasing popular demands did the Soviet leaders abandon consideration of alternative courses of action.

Reluctant Tolerance; The Costs of Control

Thus, while their reluctance to resort to military means can neither excuse nor justify what they eventually did, even the Czechoslovak case illustrates that Soviet foreign policy toward Eastern Europe has been more circumspect and ambiguous than commonly assumed; it has shown a measure of restraint and a good deal of procrastination. That it is, indeed, a curious mixture of imperious behavior combined with some tolerance toward diversity has been demonstrated time and again. For, despite Soviet displeasure, Yugoslavia, Albania and even Rumania—which, after all, refused to take part in the invasion of Czechoslovakia—remain essentially autonomous. Despite severe and public criticisms by Soviet (and East German) economists and ideologists, the far-reaching and quite liberal Hungarian economic reform has managed to survive. And despite its own repressive practices at home, the Soviet Union has long accepted the relatively tolerant attitude of successive Polish governments toward the Catholic church and toward Poland's largely independent peasants.

Needless to say, Moscow's grudging tolerance of diversity does not denote approval of pluralism, nor is the practice of military intervention precluded by the known preference of the Soviet leadership for achieving its goals by nonmilitary means. On balance, then, past Soviet performance still indicates the likelihood of continued and resolute opposition to the adaptation of Eurocommunism to Eastern Europe.

To recognize that a heavy-handed Soviet response is

likely, however, is not to suggest that it is either foreordained or foreclosed. The economic, political and ideological cost to the Soviet Union of its imperial posture in Eastern Europe is increasingly prohibitive. First, the economic cost has become such that, contrary to the pattern of the 1950s and 1960s, Eastern Europe is now an economic liability to the Soviet Union.

Given the rising price of basic commodities, especially oil, the Soviet Union has suffered large and still growing losses in its trade with Eastern Europe. By selling such commodities somewhat below world market prices and by providing a vast market for East European goods for which there is not always a ready outlet in the West or in the Third World, the Soviet Union has come to be a greater economic asset to Eastern Europe than Eastern Europe is to the Soviet Union. Second, the political cost of Moscow's hegemonic policies includes the perpetuation of deep-rooted popular discontent and high elite tension in Eastern Europe, combined with the damaging effect of such policies on the integrity of ostensibly limited and altruistic Soviet foreign-policy objectives elsewhere. Finally, the ideological cost of the Soviet imperial posture is the further alienation of the Eurocommunist parties of Western Europe that makes it ever more difficult for the Soviet leaders to recapture their leading role in world communism.

Summary: A Reversal of Influence and Initiative

Eurocommunism is not going to solve the "general crisis of communism" in Eastern Europe any more than it could solve the "general crisis of capitalism" in Western Europe. As of now, there is sufficient internal and external resistance to it on both sides of the continent to limit its influence and appeal. Should such resistance continue, the Eurocommunists will merely accelerate egalitarian trends in Western Europe toward the gradual fulfillment of social needs; in Eastern Europe, they will encourage the expansion of individual liberties. In both Eastern and Western Europe, only through the process of cooptation into existing political structures and ideologies can the Eurocommunists obtain the partial implementation of their platform.

Because authoritarian regimes seldom realize *when* they must adjust to changing conditions and *how* to make the necessary adjustments, the introduction of Eurocommunist ideas can have a far more destabilizing effect on Eastern Europe than on the relatively flexible political systems of Western Europe. Indeed, the major issue in Western Europe is not how to absorb the Eurocommunist parties' ideas, but how to maintain sufficient internal and external opposition to their residual ambition for political hegemony. For the Soviet Union and its East European supporters, on the other hand, the Eurocommunist phenomenon signifies a reversal in the flow of influence and initiative in the Communist movement, challenging the very legitimacy of their rule and offering the prospect of a Europeanization of world communism.

EUROCOMMUNISM AND THE STATE [3]

Santiago Carrillo's 218-page *Eurocommunism and the State* is the strongest written argument for Eurocommunism yet made by one of its leading proponents. The book sounds all the familiar Eurocommunist themes: independence from Moscow, democratic plurality, universal suffrage, respect for human rights. But the Spanish Communist leader goes much further: he flatly rejects the Soviet Union as a model for Western European communism, calling instead for a Socialist but democratic Western Europe that is dominated by neither the Soviet Union nor the United States. He examines the concept of the dictatorship of the proletariat and finds it undemocratic. In short, he gives the Soviets plenty to get angry about.

At the same time, Carrillo gives the West plenty to think about. He explicitly points out, for instance, that Commu-

[3] Article entitled "Quotations from Chairman Carrillo." *Time.* 110:32. Jl. 11, '77. Reprinted by permission from *Time*, the weekly newsmagazine; Copyright Time Inc. 1977.

nists must not be confused with Social Democrats, and in effect he demolishes the notion, harbored by some Western observers, that Eurocommunism is committed to peaceful change in all situations. Excerpts:

Where Moscow Went Wrong. [The Soviet invasion of Czechoslovakia in 1968] was the last straw. Any idea of internationalism ended for us . . . Progress of the Socialist movements in the developed capitalist countries would aid Soviet society and Soviet Communists in making progress in their transformation [from the present dictatorship] into an authentic workers' democracy. This is a historic necessity that would greatly benefit the cause of socialism. So it is all the more lamentable that in 1968 our Czechoslovak comrades were not allowed to continue their experiment.

Eastern Europe. Inequalities persist, there are vital problems . . . The great unresolved question survives: that of democracy and of conflicts and contradictions that a unilateral propaganda machine dissimulates but does not resolve.

Revolution. We are not returning to social democracy! . . . We do not rule out, by any means, the possibility of taking power through revolution, if the dominant classes close democratic channels and the circumstances that make revolution possible were to come about. [But in Spain today] we affirm that it is possible to go from dictatorship to democracy without force.

The Mission of Eurocommunism. Eurocommunism must show that the victory of the Socialist forces in Western Europe will not multiply Soviet power nor presuppose the extension of the one-party Soviet model. It will be an independent experience with a more advanced socialism that will have a positive influence on the democratic evolution of the [socialist models] existing today.

RADICAL CHIC: A REVIEW OF THE PRESS [4]

Many of our leading papers and magazines have lately been spreading the "news" that West European Communists have reached a point of no return in their relations with the Soviet Union, and are on the verge of becoming (or have in fact already become) democratic, pluralistic, and pro-Western. According to this view, *Eurocommunism* is well advanced along the road to independence from the Kremlin, and now threatens Brezhnev and his comrades in the Politburo with something even more menacing than the two great schisms in the history of world communism, the Titoist defection and the Sino-Soviet split. Moreover, unlike the previous ruptures, this one is held to threaten the Soviet empire in Eastern Europe, and perhaps the very structure of the Soviet Union itself.

This "news," to be sure, is hardly new. Columnists and correspondents like Tom Wicker and Anthony Lewis of the New York *Times*, Sari Gilbert and Jim Hoagland of the Washington *Post*, along with various intellectuals and would-be secretaries of state, have been spreading it for years from the lofty heights of learned foreign-policy journals and the somewhat lower altitude of diverse op-ed pages. But there are signs that the theory of an impending schism in the Communist world is gathering momentum; and since the theory is false, its rapidly growing popularity with the American press has alarming implications for American political culture and American foreign policy.

The word *Eurocommunism* was invented in 1975 by an Italian journalist who writes for Milan's anti-Communist daily *Il Giornale nuovo*, and it referred originally to the propaganda with which Enrico Berlinguer, the leader of the Italian Communist party (PCI), attempted to convince

---

[4] Article entitled "The 'News' About Eurocommunism," by Michael Ledeen, former Rome correspondent for the *New Republic*; executive editor, *Washington Review of Strategic and International Studies*; author, *The First Duce: D'Annunzio at Fiume* (Johns Hopkins, 1978). *Commentary*. 64:53–7. O. '77. Reprinted from *Commentary*, by permission; copyright © 1977 by the American Jewish Committee.

the Italian electorate that the PCI was part of the Western democratic tradition. As the word has come to be used in the American press, however, it takes this claim not as propaganda but at face value. Here, for example, are five recent definitions of Eurocommunism:

A Communist rule free of Moscow's domination, as advocated by the parties of Italy, France, and Spain, and free of the Soviet features of violent accession to power and repression to retain power (James Markham, New York *Times*, June 25).

A version of Marxism which stresses transition to socialism by parliamentary means (*Christian Science Monitor*, June 28).

Those Western Communists who had given up hope for revolution and chosen the parliamentary path to power, and, at the same time, had rejected Moscow's claim to subservience, and first loyalty as "the world's first Socialist country." . . . All three parties, though to different degrees, . . . are in favor of a national or Western defense which, put bluntly, concedes a fear of Soviet might (Flora Lewis, New York *Times*, July 3).

A mixture of socialism and Western democracy (Sari Gilbert, Washington *Post,* July 7).

A tendency in some Western Communist parties to stress independence from Moscow and opposition to coercion (Paul Hofmann, New York *Times*, July 4).

A Powder-Puff Press

As these quotations demonstrate, one hardly ever finds European Communists subjected to the sort of probing analysis or critical questioning which the New York *Times*, the Washington *Post*, *Newsweek, Time,* and the rest reserve for all other politicians, especially American ones. Thus, on July 31 [1977] the *Times* gave over an entire page to two long interviews, one with Giancarlo Pajetta of the PCI, the other with the French Communist theoretician Jean Kanapa. When Pajetta bragged of his party's reputation for "honest and capable management" in local governments, the interviewer (Ina Lee Selden) went him one better, even trying to explain away occasional failures:

The Communists do have a reputation for clean government. They have done well . . . where they inherited economically or administratively sound structures and where the population has a reputation for industry. They have been less than effective in Naples and other chronically poor southern cities.

The interview went on to reinforce the idea of Eurocommunism as "independent" of Moscow, and committed to democratic processes and Western political traditions in general.

The PCI has long been treated with kid gloves by the American press, but it is only recently that this gentle approach has been extended to Georges Marchais and his comrades in the French Communist party (PCF). In his *Times* interview with Kanapa, Paul Lewis dealt with him as indulgently as Ina Lee Selden dealt with Pajetta in the adjoining columns. The conversation with Kanapa was "a relaxing experience," and the Communist leader was allowed to present himself as a champion of human rights. "No one has suffered more from oppressive governments than the French working class," he told Lewis. "We insist on preserving the maximum of democratic liberties." The PCF, said Lewis, although "long thought of as the most rigidly orthodox and pro-Soviet in Western Europe," was now "anxious to show itself as a moderate, democratic, liberty-loving adherent of Eurocommunism."

The theme is always the same: the European Communists are committed to democracy. Moreover, this presumed Western orientation carries over into the field of foreign policy. C. L. Sulzberger of the *Times* puts it as follows:

Personally, I have been impressed in long talks with Berlinguer, and it seems to me he is being logical when he insists his party wishes at present to continue Italy's membership in NATO. . . .
The reason is that Berlinguer not only believes in developing a different form of socialism—with democratic guarantees—in his country, but also recognizes the very real possibility of a Soviet or pro-Soviet putsch in neighboring Yugoslavia some time after Tito's death.
And Berlinguer . . . doesn't fancy the idea of a Soviet or

Soviet-puppet neighbor for the independent Italy whose independent future he now . . . is helping to plan.

Sulzberger's fellow *Times* columnist, Tom Wicker, agrees:

The Italian Communist party, even in power, need not necessarily be dominated by Soviet ideology nor subservient to Soviet foreign policy. It is neither of those things now, which is one good reason for its increasing acceptability to Italian voters.

This supposed independence from the Soviet Union, both in domestic and foreign matters, is generally considered a threat to the traditional unity of the "world Communist movement." Indeed, the Western European Communists are often represented as the Protestant rebels of the Communist church. Just as Martin Luther pressed the Pope for theological reforms, so Berlinguer, Marchais, and Santiago Carrillo of the Spanish Communist party (PCE) are seen as challenging Brezhnev to change his line on a long series of questions ranging from the relations among Communist parties and countries to the treatment of dissidents and even the internal organization of the Soviet Union. Victor Zorza put forward the extreme version of the "Reformation thesis" in the Washington *Post* on June 29:

. . . some European Communists suspect that important forces in the Kremlin might welcome the break-up of the Western Communist movement. Otherwise it might emerge as a cohesive force that could press Moscow to proceed with internal reforms more in keeping with the democratic traditions to which the European Communists lay claim.

For a while, the New York *Times* editorial page maintained a certain skepticism about the genuineness of the Communists' conversion to Western values. On April 19 [1977] it warned President Carter that the West had to "gauge the democratic slogans uttered by the 'Eurocommunists'" carefully and should look for some "legitimate steps" it might take in order to "discourage their progress." By midsummer, however, the *Times*'s concern over the Communist threat to the values of Western democracy had vanished. The cause was a Soviet attack on a book by Carrillo entitled *Eurocommunism and the State*: "Why is Santiago Carrillo . . . now at the head of the Kremlin's list of public enemies?" the *Times* asked editorially on July 1. Because, it answered, "even more than his Italian and French comrades . . . Mr. Carrillo holds communism to be compatible with constitutional democracy. That means he believes there is a higher law than the will of any Communist party, even in a Communist country. . . ." [For excerpts from Carrillo's book see preceding article.]

No Democratic Socialists

Yet the plain fact is that none of the Western European Communist parties, not even the Spanish, is democratic, either in structure or in policy. Without exception, they all remain firmly committed to the rigid Leninist model of "democratic centralism" which severely limits debate within the party and enforces a harsh discipline once decisions have been taken at the top. This form of party organization is one of the major differences between the European Communist parties and the European Socialist parties—so much so that even so radical a Socialist as Olof Palme [Sweden's former prime minister] has said he would not be prepared to trust the Eurocommunists unless and until they abandoned democratic centralism. No sign of any such change can be detected in any of the Big Three—the Spanish, French, or Italian Communists.

Given the widespread assumption that Carrillo is a social democrat with a Leninist mask, it may come as a shock to some people to discover that the leader of the Spanish Communist party is not only a Leninist where internal party organization is concerned, but that he is not even committed to the rules of democratic elections. He writes in *Eurocommunism and the State*:

We are not returning to social democracy. . . . We do not rule out, by any means, the possibility of taking power through revolution, if the dominant classes close democratic channels and the circumstances that make revolution possible were to come about.

To Carrillo the electoral process is thus only a means for achieving power and not a transcendent value, as the New York *Times* and every other major American publication (with the exception of *Time*) have chosen to believe.

This rejection of the rules of the democratic game is common to all three parties. Italian party theoreticians have repeatedly stressed that the PCI views pluralism simply as a means to an end—the conquest of power—and only last January [1977] Berlinguer defiantly announced to a cheering mob in Milan that his party was not about to become social-democratic and that there would be no "Bad Godesberg" of the sort that marked the German [Social Democratic Party] SPD's acceptance of Western "bourgeois democracy." As for the French, the famous vote in 1976, by which the PCF rejected the doctrine of the "dictatorship of the proletariat" by the remarkable margin of 1,700 to zero, suggests a monolithic organization capable of producing abrupt changes in doctrine, regardless of the convictions of the party's membership. Indeed, the drastic shifts which have characterized the propaganda of the Eurocommunists of late show just how undemocratic all three parties are. As the London *Economist* has said in discussing the Carrillo affair: Mr. Carrillo has an iron grip on the Spanish party. His authoritarian control is, paradoxically, the reason he can swing the Spanish Communists solidly behind his anti-Soviet line."

The Truth About Carrillo

But what of the claim that the Eurocommunists represent a new schism in world communism? On this point there can be no doubt that Carrillo, at least, has taken the significant step of rejecting the Soviet Union as a model of communism. *Eurocommunism and the State* clearly asserts what has been common knowledge among all non-Communists for many years: that the Soviet Union is still Stalinist—a classbound, repressive society which regularly and systematically exploits the working class and can in no sense be considered the embodiment of Socialist ideals. For Carrillo, the true socialist revolution will have to be made by the Eurocommunists following a different line of development. It was because Carrillo challenged the very legitimacy of the USSR as a revolutionary society and as the leader of a revolutionary movement—and not because of his rhetorical and tactical support for democratic elections, as the *Times* would have us believe—that Brezhnev excommunicated him.

As it happens, the battle between Carrillo and the Soviet Union has been going on for nearly a decade (a fact which was, again, only mentioned in *Time*). In the late sixties the Russians even attempted to overthrow him and split the PCE by creating a loyalist Communist party under the leadership of General Enrique Lister. But in the past year and a half, Carrillo's criticism of the Kremlin has become more pointed, and again the Russians have reacted.

So far as Eurocommunism in general is concerned, however, the important point to notice is that neither the Italian nor the French party has come to Carrillo's support. Thus, in February 1977, Berlinguer refused to associate himself with Carrillo's claim that the Soviet Union is not a socialist country and told a national television audience in Italy that he could find no reason for an ideological break with the Kremlin. The following month, the much-heralded "Eurocommunist summit" was held in Madrid, in part to celebrate Carrillo's return from exile and in part to present the world with an image of an ideologically coherent and respectable Western European Communist movement. Carrillo was ready with a statement critical of the Iron Curtain countries and sympathetic to the dissidents throughout the Soviet bloc, but the French and Italians would have none of it. The Russians organized a countersummit in Sofia [Bulgaria] on the same weekend, and an Italian spokesman was quick to tell newsmen that "we have no intention of a confrontation with any of our brother countries." Then, at the end of April, Marchais came to Rome to meet with Berlinguer, but again no word of criticism of the Kremlin was uttered. In June, when Brezhnev launched his attack against Carrillo, there was no protest from the PCI or PCF. The

Italians lamented the "tone" of the Kremlin's criticism, but had nothing to say about the content of Carrillo's ideas—which was the real issue. The French were virtually silent on the question, muttering nationalistic slogans about their continued "independence." At the end of June, a three-man PCI delegation went to Moscow and returned proclaiming that the PCI "continued to be part of a great international movement." There was no criticism of the Soviet system and no defense of Carrillo. Carrillo himself was quite explicit, telling a friend that *"Berlinguer ha fallado,"* the PCI Secretary had failed him in his hour of need.

Foreign Policy: USSR Carbons

But if Carrillo is the only Eurocommunist leader to have broken with the Russians on the issue of the nature of Soviet society, *no* Eurocommunist party, including the Spanish, has broken with the Kremlin on issues of foreign policy. Contrary to the claims of Wicker, Zorza, and their ilk, there is a virtual identity between the foreign policies of the Western European Communists and the Soviet Union on all matters involving the struggle between democracy and totalitarianism. Carrillo is violently anti-American and rarely departs from the *Pravda* line on international affairs. Marchais, the "Gaullocommunist," has never been a great supporter of the Western alliance (he wants French missiles aimed at America). Italian Communists steadfastly deny even the vaguest possibility that the West is threatened by Soviet power, and just this past May [1977], one of their leaders, Ugo Pecchioli, told [journalist] Rowland Evans that while American domination of Western Europe was a serious problem, he saw "no element of Soviet imperialism in Eastern Europe."

The Eurocommunists (again including Carrillo) stand with the Soviet Union on issue after issue: Cubans in Angola are "freedom fighters" while pro-Western Angolans are "imperialists." The Israeli liberation of Jewish hostages at Entebbe airport is branded "an intolerable violation of Ugandan national sovereignty." After years of supporting

Somalia, the Big Three suddenly shift to the side of Ethiopia—along with the same change in the Soviet strategy. [See "Somalia: Changing of the Guard" in Section II, above.] NATO itself is singled out for particular criticism by the "pro-NATO" PCI which, in fact, continually says that although it would not wish to take Italy out of the alliance, it would work to change NATO's pro-American, anti-Soviet character.

A Menace to the Kremlin?

Yet despite the undeviating support the Eurocommunists give to the Soviet foreign-policy line, the press—in keeping with its view of the "schism" with the Kremlin—continues to claim that Eurocommunism potentially or even actually represents an anti-Soviet force in world affairs. Victor Zorza says that the Russians are alarmed at the prospect of a "European Communist foreign policy that might take an anti-Soviet direction," and *Time* suspects that "Moscow's deepest concern is probably the possible reverberations that Eurocommunism, if allowed to develop unchecked, might have among the captive regimes of Eastern Europe." The New York *Times* concurs:

It is the idea that threatens the Soviet regime . . . the idea is an even greater threat to the Soviet-sponsored regimes of Poland, Hungary, Czechoslovakia, and East Germany which have all faced similar demands from their peoples, including Communists. . . . Once it is acknowledged that Communists may be challenged and defeated at the polls by non-Communist or even rival Communist parties, and that citizens enjoy rights of speech and assembly beyond those granted them by a ruling Communist oligarchy, there would remain no ideological defense for the East European dictatorships and not much difference between Europe's Communist and Socialist parties.

This theory has now achieved something approaching universal acceptance, even—if Bernard Gwertzman of the New York *Times* is correct—among some in the Carter Administration:

. . . some officials assert privately that over a long period the evolution of independent, more democratic Communist parties, such as that in Spain, might not be a negative phenomenon.

They said that, in historical terms, if the Western European Communist parties evolved into democratic bodies and were legitimately willing to take part in free elections, this could have a major influence in eroding the Soviet Union's hold in Eastern Europe and the Soviet Communist party itself.

In other words, if the West European Communists ceased to be Communists and turned into social democrats, the captive nations of the Soviet empire would discover that life is better without Russian tanks and COMECON rationing. As though the people of Poland, Hungary, East Germany, and Czechoslovakia—who revolted against the Kremlin at a time when there was not the slightest hint of heresy from Rome, Paris, and Madrid—needed Carrillo, Marchais, and Berlinguer to make them hate their Soviet taskmasters, and as though the Soviet empire were held together by anything other than Soviet tanks!

Along with the notion that Eurocommunism menaces the Kremlin goes the complementary view that it is a movement which is good for the West. Tom Wicker, for example, while admitting that the entry of the PCI into the Italian government might easily produce the disintegration of NATO, argues that this is not so very important:

. . . a substantial body of opinion doesn't think American forces in Europe contribute all that much to fundamental Western security anyway. And if new structures of Western security have to be built or old ones adapted because of European political developments, that may be easier than trying to forestall those developments with American threats and CIA money.

That is to say, the destruction of the Atlantic alliance is a small enough price to pay for the success of Eurocommunism, which Wicker believes is clearly in the best long-term interests of the West:

. . . an Italian government with Communist participation might well bring that country more prosperity and stability. Is Italian stability good for Western security, or should we prefer continuing economic chaos and political paralysis under the discredited Christian Democrats?

But the truth of the matter, of course, is that Eurocommunism is a threat to the West and hardly menaces the Soviet Union at all. It is a threat to the West because it represents a new tactic in the unremitting effort to lull the democratic world into the belief that it has nothing to fear from the spread of communism. This is, paradoxically, one of the major explanations for Russian ambivalence about the rapid growth in the strength of the Western European Communist parties. The Soviets worry that a premature entry of the Eurocommunists into government might rekindle Western anxieties and therefore also Western resolve to resist both the undermining of democracy from within and the external threat to the security of the democratic world embodied in the massive Soviet military buildup and the adventurist foreign policy of the Kremlin. To be sure, the Russians are also concerned about the possibility that Carrillo's heretical ideas might spread to France and Italy, but events have demonstrated that this is highly unlikely. It is the threat of a Western response to communism that is far more alarming to Brezhnev and his comrades.

The Dream of a "Third Force"

The fact that so many of our leading papers and magazines insist that a major schism has either occurred or is about to take place can be understood in the context of a long search by Western intellectuals for a viable alternative to American-style capitalist democracy on the one side and Soviet-style totalitarian communism on the other. This dream of a "third force" was, ironically, once attached to Italian fascism. During the twenties (though many would prefer to forget it), Mussolini was widely hailed throughout the democratic countries in much the same terms reserved these days for Berlinguer, and it took more than a decade before Italian fascism began to be revealed as a mortal danger to Western civilization. After World War II, the dream of an independent third force came to rest with the social democrats, but after thirty years of exercising power in many European countries, the Socialist parties have lost their glamor. European socialism now appears too bland, too "bourgeois" to carry the burden of a vision of a radical alternative which is capable of transforming the world.

Today, improbable as it once would have seemed, the West European Communist parties are being cast in the role of the third force—a radical socialism free of any trace of Stalinism and as independent of Moscow as it is of Washington. That the Communists are badly miscast in this role ought to be obvious to everyone, especially journalists whose job it is to expose just such tendentious political illusions. Instead, the press has all too often been the mouthpiece and propagator of these illusions, parroting the rhetoric in which our enemies become our friends, our defeats become victories, and our weakness becomes strength.

Orwell was clearly a better prophet than even his greatest admirers have thought: judging from the American press, we are ahead of his schedule by a full seven years.

A DEBATE BETWEEN TWO LEFTS [5]

The paradox of the concept of Eurocommunism is undoubtedly the combination of its extraordinary success in the United States and the skeptical treatment it has met since its birth in Europe in the countries concerned. European political commentators, including this author, noted in 1975 how difficult it was to apply the same concept to situations so different as the Italian one, where a powerful Communist party was allied to a powerful conservative party in order for the two of them to monopolize political life; the French one, where, in contrast, an important, though not dominant, Communist party allied itself to the Socialists and cut the political world into two irreconcilable halves; or the Spanish or Portuguese situations, where two minor Communist parties (about 10 percent of the vote)

[5] From article "The Myths of Eurocommunism," by Jean-François Revel, author of Without Marx or Jesus and The Totalitarian Temptation, columnist for L'Express. Foreign Affairs. 56:295–305. Ja. '78. Reprinted by permission from Foreign Affairs, January 1978. Copyright 1977 by Council on Foreign Relations, Inc.

had more coverage than their actual weight justified: the Spanish, because it presented the most liberal image in the Western world and risked nothing by doing so; and, on the other hand, the Portuguese, by trying with the help of the army to establish a dictatorship in the purest Leninist style.

The "Death of Eurocommunism"?

The point at which Europeans had little confidence in the solidity of Eurocommunism was evident from the moment that the first cracks appeared in the Union of the French Left, in September 1977. The explanation that immediately came to the minds of the Socialist analysts, when they perceived the incomprehensible hardening of the French Communist party, was the influence of Moscow. These are the same people who for five years had been maintaining that French communism had completely detached itself from Russian communism, and then decided from one day to the next to perceive the hand of the Kremlin in the crisis of the French Left. The noted Paris daily, *Le Monde*, which for years had been the most ardent defender of the thesis of the independence of the French Communist party from the USSR, published in rapid succession two articles, "The French Communist Party and Proletarian Internationalism" and "The Hand of Moscow," both of which attributed the change of course of the French Communists to Leonid Brezhnev. While it is true that they left question marks, until quite recently *Le Monde* would have considered the mere question itself to be sacrilegious. Nowadays, articles and declarations proliferate in Italy, in France and in Spain, proclaiming "the death of Eurocommunism" and adding "if it ever existed." François Mitterrand [France], Alvaro Cunhal [Portugal], Felipe Gonzalez [Spain] and Giorgio Amendola [Italy] all agree on this point.

On the other hand, during my visits to the United States in 1975, 1976 and 1977, I saw to what degree one is suspect by the academic and the liberal press Establishment if one retains a critical attitude in regard to Eurocommunism or, indeed, to communism in general. According to the current

cliché, it means "a return to the cold war." American
liberals do not understand the existence in Europe, and in
France and Italy in particular, of a violent anti-Communist
Left among people who were only twenty in 1970 or even
1975 and who have not lived through the cold war and do
not even know what it is. The explosion of the "new phi-
losophers" in France, the mass demonstrations of the extra-
parliamentary extreme Left in Italy fall into this category
(together with many members of the preceding generation,
who have not been conditioned by the cold war). The Communist phenomenon, including what I have called . . .
"unofficial Stalinism," should be examined independently
and not in relation to other concepts, such as the "cold
war" or "McCarthyism," which are today without any se-
mantic content.

"Democratic Centralism"

For instance, to ask oneself whether the West European
Communist parties have remained Stalinist is not a matter
to be resolved by a vague evaluation or by impressions
gathered through personal contacts with French or Italian
Communists or by a subjective confidence in their writings,
promises or declarations. On the contrary, it is a technical
problem: as long as the Western Communist parties remain
organized according to the so-called schema of "democratic
centralism," meaning a Politburo, recruited by cooptation,
which nominates and controls from top to bottom the members of the Central Committee and the federation secretaries, the sections, and lastly the cells, and consequently all
the delegates to the congresses, it is ridiculous to speak of
de-Stalinization. Actually, this structure adheres strictly—and
has always done so—to the Stalinist-Leninist organization
of the Communist party. It transforms the deliberations of
the rank and file into phony discussions, completely pre-
fabricated by the Politburo. This results in a ritual "unanimous" vote of the Central Committees of the parties. Indeed,
the French and the Italian parties have never ceased to
function in accordance with this schema. And this leads one

to ask the following question: if, tomorrow, in France, coalition governments were to include Communist ministers, whose orders would these Communist ministers obey? The prime minister's? The president of the republic's? or those of the Politburo of their party? In the current state of things, the answer is: the Politburo's. This is incompatible with the practice of a representative democracy and with the constitution, precisely because the Communist party works in an undemocratic and oligarchic way. This technical angle is the only one that makes it possible to see things clearly: all the rest is literature and impressionistic gossip.

To take another example: independence from Moscow. It is impossible to know absolutely the degree and method used by Moscow to control the Western Communist parties. But one thing can be measured with precision because it consists of public and published declarations, i.e., the extent of the support of the Italian and the French Communist parties for Russia's foreign policy. Has there been, since 1975, one or several aspects of Soviet foreign policy toward which a Western Communist party has adopted a reserved or critical attitude? The answer is simple: none. Whether it be Angola, Mozambique, the Polisario liberation front [a guerrilla movement, aided by Algeria, that proclaimed the Spanish Sahara region independent in 1976], the conflict between Ethiopia and Somalia, the Helsinki agreements, Israel, the civil war in Lebanon, Communist newspapers and Communist leaders in the West have approved wholly and unconditionally Soviet theories and behavior. It is not a question of mysterious secret ties between Moscow and the Western Communist parties but of historical fact.

The Anti-Communist Left

Certainly there are other elements to be taken into account: the condemnation of the Soviet intervention in Czechoslovakia by the Italian Communist party or the pledge by both the Italian and French parties to remain within the Atlantic Alliance. In these two cases, however, one must examine not the propaganda value but the substance of these declarations. The Western Communist parties claim that they condemn the excesses of Soviet repression but simultaneously have launched a fantastic campaign of intimidation and calumny against [Russian dissenters] Solzhenitsyn, Andrei Amalrik and Vladimir Bukovsky. They say they want to stay in the Atlantic Alliance (the Italians even in NATO) but French Communist Jean Kanapa's report on the defense policy of the French Communist party results in the isolation of France within the Atlantic system and, thus, in the dismantling of the Alliance. This serves "objectively" Soviet interests, the principal designated enemy being West Germany! It is not surprising that [Socialist] François Mitterrand has described the new Communist doctrine in defense matters as ludicrous and that it has been one of the main points of the conflict in the crisis between Socialists and Communists in France.

Here are some examples of diagnosis and of concrete questions, which are really the only way of dealing with Eurocommunism. By contrast, to deal with it, as is frequently done, by generalizing leads to utter confusion. And, above all, the evolution of the Communist phenomenon in the world should not be confused with the evolution of the psychological attitude of Americans toward communism.

In the 1950s, communism was much less powerful and widespread than it is today. The Soviet regime was isolated in its geographical sphere and the inferiority of its economy, its military forces and its technology. The riots and the staged trials in the satellite countries and the revelations on Stalinism by Khrushchev in 1956 had discredited it. Cuba was not Communist. Southeast Asia was not Communist. That vast portions of Africa could, one day, become subject to the direct or indirect influence of the Soviet Union was unthinkable. It was also inconceivable that West European Communist parties might accede to power either by electoral means or by revolution.

At that time, however, Americans saw the Communist danger everywhere. Any European who tried to explain to them the existence in Europe of a long tradition of non-Communist, nontotalitarian socialism and stressed the necessity of understanding this would himself be accused of being a Communist. Even worse, if he explained that the large number of Communist voters in Italy or in France was not entirely due to the machinations of the KGB but had, instead, national roots that one had to analyze, he was considered an active propagandist of communism.

Today, even though communism exists on all continents and the influence of unofficial Stalinism overlaps the actual Communist sphere and penetrates even Britain's Labour party, we witness the opposite phenomenon. Americans no longer see totalitarian danger anywhere when it is present everywhere. Only détente and Eurocommunism are respectable and accepted at their face value. (One could go back even further to observe this curious Anglo-American swing: sometimes everyone is suspected of Communist sympathies, sometimes no Communist is considered dangerous. On May 23, 1943, the New York *Times* published an article stating that the Russians were changing the structures of their economy and progressively abandoning communism. *Fortune* [April 1943] believed that after the war the USSR would be too weak to expand in Europe, even ideologically. Finally, the dissolution of the Comintern was hailed by *The Times* of London [May 24, 1943] as one of the most important events of the war and proof that the Russians would not try to influence central Europe after peace. The monumental naiveté of these assertions need hardly be stressed today.) American liberals, and even nonliberals, have retained from the 1950s the idea, or rather the conditioned reflex, that the rejection of communism is always a conservative stance. This is completely wrong. In Europe, the most uncompromising anti-Communists have always been the Socialists, the large social-democratic parties of Germany, Scandinavia, the Netherlands, Austria and Great Britain (before the current "Marxization" of its left wing). To this very traditional anti-Communist Left have recently been added the young antitotalitarian radicals I have mentioned

above. In this context, the experiment of an alliance between the French Communist party and the Socialist party
of François Mitterrand is not the rule but the exception,
and (as the mishaps of the alliance seem to indicate) an unfortunate exception. In general, it has contributed more to
the Finlandization of the Socialist party than to the democratization of the Communist party. Hence, it is profoundly
unfair and wrong to consider all the skeptical reactions to
Eurocommunism as coming solely from the Right.

The fundamental controversy about Eurocommunism in
Europe is thus not a debate between the Right and the
Left but between two Lefts. The question is which trend of
European socialism—the Leninist or the social-democratic—
will prevail.

Let us now return to what is, in theory, the substance of
Eurocommunism, so that we can then ask ourselves if it is
viable or even if it exists. Eurocommunism defines itself, in
the first instance, as a demand by the Communist parties for
independence from Moscow and hence the right to define,
at home, "their national road toward socialism." Further, it
defines itself by a desire for democratization on the part of
the Western Communist parties and for respect for the law,
both in the struggle for and in the exercise of power. Communists promise, in particular, to give up power if they lose
the elections (provided there are any).

These two points—de-Russification and pluralistic democracy—must be examined in turn according to two criteria.

Old Wine

First, are the themes of Eurocommunism new? It is important to know if this is so because Eurocommunism has
been presented as a decisive, indeed an irreversible innovation, of Western communism. Second, to what extent do the
words and deeds of the Western Communist parties coincide? It is important to measure this, because, curiously, although Communist leaders in every country have lied far
more than anybody since the beginning of politics (even
more than Hitler who, after all, announced his intentions

quite clearly in *Mein Kampf*), it is virtually sacrilegious today to doubt their promises. Skepticism in regard to electoral promises of any political party is considered in democracies as a prudent and an elementary right of the citizen; however, the exercise of this right, when it comes to Eurocommunists, is considered (and, at the risk of repeating myself, especially in the United States) as the irrefutable sign of a conservative mentality.

To test whether or not the Eurocommunist Communist parties are truly independent in relation to the USSR and if this is a new phenomenon, one must keep in mind the following principles.

1. The relations between non-Soviet Communist parties, in or out of power, and Moscow have never been without problems. The history of the Communist movement is full of cases of leaders who did not think the policy that Moscow wanted to impose was suitable for local conditions. Between 1956 and 1964, for instance, the French Communist party was constantly hostile to Khrushchev and plotted with the "Molotov group" of old-line Stalinists. On the other hand, the Italians, who had previously been in veiled disagreement with Moscow, supported Khrushchev ardently. It is difficult to interpret the real relationship because secrecy reigns over the Communist world. For instance, the Italian Communist party is now by far the Western party that enjoys the best relations with Moscow. *Pravda* does not miss an occasion to praise Enrico Berlinguer, although logically he should be the most detested leader, since he presumably launched the Eurocommunist wave. At the Eurocommunist summit in Madrid, in March 1977, Enrico Berlinguer was the man who insisted that the final statement contain no mention of human rights in the USSR. And let us not forget that before the 1948 breach, the Yugoslav party was the most pro-Soviet of European parties.

2. The programs of "national democratic unions" and of popular fronts demanding "original paths toward socialism" reappear periodically in the history of Communist parties, especially of those that are not, or not yet, com-

pletely in power. In 1946, Klement Gottwald declared before the Czechoslovak Central Committee: "There is not just one road to socialism, there is not just the path that passes through the dictatorship of the proletariat and the Soviets. Another road to socialism can be envisaged." Maurice Thorez, secretary general of the French Communist party, in an interview given to *The Times* of London on November 18, 1946, declared: "The progress of democracy throughout the world, despite those rare exceptions that prove the rule, permits other roads to socialism than the one followed by Russian Communists." In the same year, Mathias Rakosi for Hungary, and Georgi Dimitrov for Bulgaria offered numerous reassurances in the same style: different ways toward communism exist and "there will be no dictatorship of the proletariat." These were the periods of the great alliances: Communist ministers were members of the French and of the Italian governments, with Christian-Democrats, Socialists and Gaullists. These alliances were also broken overnight. As for the countries of Central Europe, one knows the nature of the regimes they were rapidly subjected to (including Czechoslovakia, from 1948 on, *without any intervention by the Soviet army*).

3. Until now, Communist strategies have always been reversible. . . . We have seen in France this past September [1977] how a sudden hardening of the Communist party can, with one stroke, reverse a policy followed for years. . . .

4. Even when the [French] "Marchais line" and the [Italian] "Berlinguer line" give formal endorsement to a certain autonomy, the governing bodies of the French and Italian parties always include members close to the Soviet leadership, ready to take over if necessary. The same is true of the Communist unions, like the CGT [Confédération Générale du Travail] in France.

Moscow's Economic Sponsorship

5. The financial relations between Moscow and the non-Soviet Communist parties no longer consist of direct payments, as in former times, except in the case of the

small parties (Denmark, the Netherlands, Norway, etc.). But in Italy and in France financial relations do exist by way of commissions on commerce between East and West received by import-export companies independent in legal form from any political party but actually owned by straw men of the Communist parties. The most famous one in France is a company by the name of Interagra, headed by the "Communist billionaire," Jean-Baptiste Doumeng, which has the monopoly on French commerce with the East in wine, meat, cereals and butter. There are other companies of the same sort for manufactured goods. No French or Italian producer, who wants to sell to the East, can ever obtain a contract without going through one of these middlemen. This largely explains the wealth of the French and of the Italian Communist parties, which paradoxically are the two richest political parties in their countries, although the contributions of the registered members (500,000 in France, 1,500,000 in Italy, not to be confused with voters) are very far from explaining this wealth.

Consequently it is quite obvious that if the USSR ever considered Eurocommunists as its enemies, it would put a stop to this considerable source of profits. By the same token, the Western Communist parties can hardly afford the luxury of breaking completely with the Russians, even when they find them difficult to put up with. One can sometimes be on very bad terms with Moscow without breaking with Moscow, as one can sometimes be on very bad terms with one's wife or husband without divorcing.

6. Eurocommunists have never stopped totally supporting the foreign policy of the Soviet Union (as has already been mentioned above).

To conclude: there have always been periods of affirmation of "national roads" followed by periods of avowed obedience to Moscow. For example, in France, the national road and the popular front from 1935 to 1939; return to Moscow with the Russo-German Pact; and, during national or Eurocommunist periods, relations with the Soviet party are never broken. Thus, between 1935 and 1939, Maurice Thorez had his independent policy dictated to him by an agent of the Comintern who stayed at his side and whose name and activity is now known: Eugen Fried. . . .

The Question of Control

Notwithstanding all the reservations that I have made above, *the right to criticize* the present regime in the USSR and the other East European states has certainly been clearly established since 1968 and particularly since the publication of *The Gulag Archipelago* [Solzhenitsyn's account of the Soviet forced labor camps]. The Western Communist parties had to separate their image from that of the USSR, which had become simply too repulsive. Whenever the question "Where would you want to live if you had to leave France?" was asked in polls, hardly 2 percent of Communist voters would answer "in the USSR." In October 1977, the French Communist party condemned unequivocally the parody-like trial in Prague of certain dissidents. But, at the same time, the French Communist party never ceased approving as authentically Socialist the foundations of the Soviet system, particularly its economic base. Proving themselves to be bad Marxists, French Communists do not ask themselves how an economic system can be fundamentally good and liberating if sixty years of police-state terror has been necessary in order to enforce it.

Above all, the essential point that I want to make here is the following: even if the Western Communist parties were to go to the point of breaking openly with Moscow, which *is* possible, it would not mean that they had become, in a domestic context, democratic parties. *De-Russification is not democratization.* The Communist parties of Yugoslavia, China and Albania have broken with the Soviet Communist party, but they have maintained and even aggravated the totalitarian system. The most totalitarian of all the popular democracies of Eastern Europe is Rumania, which as a nation-state is the one that least follows Soviet foreign policy. Nonalignment is a concept that has to do with the will of the leadership to be all-powerful and not with the will of the people to be free. The present Cambodian leaders are nonaligned, despite the recent courtesy visit of Pol Pot [Saloth Sar, Cambodian political leader] to Peking. . . .

The Causes of Eurocommunism

Eurocommunism may be defined, then, as the result of two phenomena that have occurred over the last twenty years. First, the realization in Western Europe of the economic and human failure of Soviet socialism. This realization is not quite clear yet but it is no longer possible to suggest the "Soviet paradise" as a goal and a model for Western voters. Second, the adaptation of the Communist parties to advanced industrial societies—or rather, their clumsy efforts to "direct" these societies without renouncing their principles. . . .

The first phenomenon enabled the Communist parties to have a much freer hand in dealing with their particular situations. If we take the Spanish party, for instance, we must keep in mind that its extraordinary good will comes from the atrocious image it had given the Left as a result of its behavior during the Civil War. It fought the Civil War for itself and for the Soviet Union within the Republican camp, against the Anarchists and the Socialists far more than against Franco. It had to purify its image at any price.

The second phenomenon—the increasing complication of the social structure of societies enriched by industrial and post-industrial development—forces the Communist parties to confront a dilemma: remain revolutionary parties and take power illegally or take power legally and blend into social democracy. Eurocommunism can be logical and coherent only if it results in the disappearance of communism. This is the reason why its short history is already filled with illogicalities, contradictions and reversals. Nothing, however, makes it possible to believe that Communists do not have as their goal, today as yesterday, the monopoly of power.

V. ITALY: A CASE STUDY

EDITOR'S INTRODUCTION

As the Western European country with the strongest Communist party—one that has considerable strength at the local level—Italy has come to special attention in discussions of Eurocommunism. This section takes a closer look at Italy as embodying situations and problems that may occur in other countries if Communists gain power and become, as they are there, of pivotal importance, not only in national party politics but in daily, local administration on the municipal level. What will be the effect on the political future of Italy of the government's firm stand in the face of the Red Brigade's kidnapping of Aldo Moro, their demands for the release of political prisoners, and the subsequent killing of the captive former prime minister? Can the Christian Democrats, Socialists, and Communists continue to field a viable government?

The opening selection, from *Time* magazine, describes the political compromise that has been holding the country together and some of the common measures that the government and its Communist partners have taken. A New York *Times* article follows, noting the Communist party's more recent demand for a greater voice in the government. The article also discusses the workings of the party; its attitudes toward dissenters of various kinds, conservative and radical; its performance in local administration; and views of its policies should it achieve greater power.

Next, author Mauro Lucentini, American correspondent for the Milan *Giornale nuovo*, looks at Communists in administration from another perspective: the growth of the public sector, its relationship to private industry, and its implications for the Communist-conservative coalition and Communist rule.

Finally, a *Time* magazine critique of the Communist

party from the viewpoint of the militant Left describes tensions and attitudes that resulted in the abduction and subsequent murder of Aldo Moro in 1978—attitudes that charge the party with collusion with bourgeoisie.

NEARER THE "HISTORIC COMPROMISE" [1]

Was it [the coalition of Christian Democrats and Communists] a step toward the "historic compromise" that Italy's Communists have long dreamed of—a coalition government that could lead to all-out Communist control? Or was it merely a temporary liaison—a "seaside compromise," as some Italians were calling it?

After fourteen weeks and sixty-one formal sessions, the country's major parties had reached an agreement for a common program to reinforce Premier Giulio Andreotti's minority government. The Christian Democrats were relieved to have their tenuous hold on power strengthened, and the Communists were pleased because the deal gave them a formal voice in government policy for the first time in thirty years.

For the moment at least, the agreement appeared to resolve the curious impasse under which Andreotti has governed since last year's election. The Christian Democrats won 39 percent of the vote and 263 of the 630 seats in the Chamber of Deputies (v. 34 percent and 228 seats for the Communists), and were unable to put together a majority coalition. Ever since, Andreotti has governed with the tacit support of the Communists and other major parties, who have consistently abstained on confidence votes. But . . . [in] spring [1977] both the Communists and the Socialists (10 percent of the popular vote and 57 seats) demanded a more direct voice in government policy.

The Communists and Socialists first demanded a whole new governing majority. In the end they settled for a series of agreements with the Christian Democrats on specific points of policy:

[1] Article in *Time*. 110:33. Jl. 11, '77. Reprinted by permission from *Time*, the weekly newsmagazine; Copyright Time Inc. 1977.

☐ To combat rising crime the Communists agreed to extend the powers of the police to interrogate suspects and detain them without charges for forty-eight hours.

☐ To fight inflation (now running at 19 percent and meet the terms of a big IMF [International Monetary Fund] loan, the parties agreed to curb spending and freeze government hiring.

☐ To help bail out deficit-ridden municipal governments, many of which are run by the Communists and Socialists, the Christian Democrats agreed to support a package of new local taxes.

Both sides faced risks. By helping the Andreotti regime stay in power the Communists risked antagonizing their own Left wing, not to mention the extreme Left splinter groups (including many students). The Christian Democrats, who had always vowed not to form a partnership with the Communists, could alienate some support if they seemed now to be reneging on that promise. But Andreotti said he thought the agreement "refutes the theory that Italy is ungovernable." Communist leader Enrico Berlinguer called it "a forward step" that gave the country a badly needed "breath of relief."

Washington and many of Italy's other Western allies feared that the deal might amount to a psychological breakthrough for the Italian Communists. But for the moment the United States seemed prepared to accept the conventional view that the agreement was a successful trade-off. "Each side," observed one Italian cabinet official, "allowed the other to save face, knowing that in politics it is a mistake to over-win."

BERLINGUER PRACTICES A GUIDED DEMOCRACY [2]

The Italian Communist party . . . seemed closer . . . [in early February 1978] to its avowed goal: sharing power in

[2] From an article by Paul Hofmann, staff correspondent. New York *Times*. sec. IV, p E 4. F. 12, '78. © 1978 by The New York Times Company. Reprinted by permission.

the central government with No. 1, the Christian Democrats. It now appears to be a question of semantics, rather
than substance, that has to be worked out before the Communists will have a peripheral say in how the country is run.
Would it have made much difference if they had a more
formal role with such minor portfolios as the post office and
the merchant marine?

Some prominent Italians don't think it would matter.
Ugo La Malfa, leader of the small but influential Republican party who has been a member of several governments
and has long professed anti-Communist views, asserts the
Italian Communist party has changed. He says it has become
liberalized and is needed to resolve the country's grave difficulties. However, the Christian Democratic party has
steadily denied the Communists a direct part in the government.

The difference in attitude results from a different per-
ception of the leadership, ideology and allegiance of the
Italian Communists. For example, the determination of the
Christian Democrats to bar the Communist party from what
Italians call the Room of the Pushbuttons—an imaginary
national power center—arises from uneasiness over the
party's real nature, ultimate aims and true relationship with
Moscow. The Christian Democrats have never really believed that Enrico Berlinguer and his colleagues are intent
on following national Italian not international Communist
policies.

Other political leaders believe differently, and, to take
advantage of this potential base of support, the Communist
party . . . [in January 1978] offered a deliberate show of
internal democracy, permitting the 176-member Central
Committee to discuss political strategy openly. To nobody's
surprise, the committee reconfirmed the party's earlier bid
for participation in a "national emergency government."
But the debate was only embroidery for a political line that
had already been fixed by the party's inner councils, the
secretariat and the directorate, which retain the real power.

Only Tactics Differ

These groups consist of fewer than a dozen men—no women—with Mr. Berlinguer, the sad-faced secretary general, acting as a referee among associates who may differ on tactics but appear in basic agreement on long-term targets. These objectives, many Italians suggest, are the conquest of power, step by little step, and the transformation of Italian society according to a still somewhat vague "Socialist" model.

Mr. Berlinguer's position rests essentially on his control of the party apparatus. The secretary general is the supreme bureaucrat, a creature of the apparatus, rather than a charismatic leader. The Italian Communist party's "internal democracy" does not allow organized dissent. When a group of party intellectuals advocated a more radical course a few years ago, it was forced out of the party and is now an independent left-wing group known as the Manifesto. In an address to the Central Committee . . . [in January 1978], Mr. Berlinguer again called for mopping up "radical-extremist" pockets in the rank and file. But clearly intent on allaying misgivings, he emphasized his party's commitment to democratic methods.

There have been some examples of this tolerance of views critical of workers' rights or wider Communist policy. A few days ago, a Communist labor leader, Luciano Lama, startled workers by telling them they must step up productivity, contain their wage demands and curb absenteeism. Umberto Terracini, a cofounder of the party who under the Fascist dictatorship spent seventeen years in prison, recently remarked that the Soviet Union "is completely devoid of any freedom." Mr. Terracini was not ousted from the party directorate for the remark; he has long been a tolerated maverick without power. For some time, the Italian Communist press has been mildly critical of human rights violations in the Soviet Union and its satellites. Mr. Berlinguer himself has stressed at international Communist rallies and again in Rome . . . [in January] that the Italian road toward socialism was different from the Soviet road.

Local Government

More than half of Italy's 56 million people have had direct experience with Communists in local government. Generally, Communists have proved to be competent and honest administrators. True, the Communist performance in local government is much more impressive in such a showcase city as Bologna where the party has been in power since the end of World War II than in Rome which has had a pro-Communist mayor . . . [since August 1976] or in dilapidated Naples. As councilmen, city commissioners, mayors and regional presidents Communists work smoothly within the system that the party's ideologists routinely denounce as capitalistic and excessively consumer-oriented. Where Communists are locally in power, they have often shown consideration for the views of the conservative opposition. They woo church-going Roman Catholics. The party that represents one of every three Italian voters and, with 1.8 million cardholders, is the strongest Communist movement in the West is in many ways already operating as part of the nation's power structure.

But former Communists who have left the party and political scientists who have studied it closely say its core is not really different from the small Leninist cliques that make all decisions in the Communist parties of Eastern Europe. A recent study by an Italian analyst, Giuseppe Are, found the party "authoritarian and centralized." But Professor Are conceded that the leadership was sensitive to the moods of the membership.

However, there is no instance of any serious divergence between the Italian Communist party and Moscow on international issues. Mr. Berlinguer's party backs Soviet policies in the Middle East, Africa and elsewhere. It says it can live with Italian membership in the Atlantic alliance, but Italian Communist leaders are reticent in discussing the subject.

The close ties between the Italian Communist leadership and the Soviet Union became again apparent early . . . [in January 1978] when a Berlinguer aide, Giovanni Cervetti, went to Moscow to brief top Soviet officials, including the

influential Andrei P. Kirilenko, on the Italian situation.
An Italian diplomat who has served in Eastern Europe
observed . . . "Sure, Italian communism has evolved over
the last several years. If it were to seize power, it might be
expected to build a society somewhat resembling present-
day Hungary rather than Czechoslovakia or the Soviet
Union." The diplomat quoted the dictum of Janos Kadar,
the Hungarian Communist chief: "Anyone who is not
against us is for us." Mr. Berlinguer could have said that, he
remarked and then added, "like Kadar, Berlinguer would
be a comparatively liberal ruler. Italian film makers could
still shoot bawdy movies and artists paint abstract pictures.
Some Italians might still be able to travel abroad. Priests
would still be paid by the state. Italians would still eat well.
But the nation would drift into the eastern orbit and the
party would never vacate the Room of the Pushbuttons."

THE NEW CLASS [3]

Italy, the poorest and the least productive of Western
industrial nations, has a public payroll that is, in proportion
to its population, ten times as large as that of the United
States; parts of its bureaucracy are incredibly well paid,
with secretaries in some branches of government getting
salaries of $30,000. Italy's journalists, most of whom work
for a government-subsidized press, are possibly the best paid
in the world. More than half of the total Italian labor force
has already retired on official pension plans. Some 25,000
state agencies exist solely for the purpose of supporting a
government-produced clientele. Most Italian art, most Italian education, most of Italian culture is financed by the
government and serviced by political protégés. Over the
last fifteen years, in short, Italy has become the first major
Western country to produce a New Class of the kind first

[3] Article by Mauro Lucentini, author, American correspondent of the Milan
paper *Il Giornale nuovo*, an independent daily founded by former writers for
Il Corriere della sera. Commentary. 63:48–50. N. '76. Reprinted from *Commentary*, by permission; copyright © 1976 by the American Jewish Committee.

described by the Yugoslav intellectual Milovan Djilas: a self-appointed, self-serving state elite.

All this has been brought about by the close cooperation of the Communists and the dominating left wings of the government parties. Both Communists and non-Communists have formed the New Class, even though the former have until now been underrepresented in it. At the moment, the entry of the Communists into the government at the national level (they already share in government at the local level and in parliament) is being resisted by an ever-weakening faction within the government parties, fighting an uphill battle. But Italy is already deeply "socialized" —most of its economy is already in government hands and the rest is subject to untold government controls and pressures; moreover, all forms of expression and of cultural life in Italy already march to the tune of left-wing values. A "shift" to communism, then, would not introduce a radically new situation; it would lead to the further erosion and possible disappearance of freedoms that are already restricted. The access of the Communists to national government would constitute only the last phase of a process that has gone on for a long time: a phase wherein, the economy having collapsed, an authoritarian intervention would become necessary to save the privileges of the New Class. Only the Communist party has the political freshness, the cultural aura, and the international support necessary to perform this function.

The way in which two ostensible enemies, the government and the Communist party, have managed to cooperate in the last fifteen years in the interest of a common New Class is a miracle of political subtlety, even for Italian politics with its notorious arcana. Yet the objectives of cooperation have all along been straightforward and clear: first, to transfer assets from private hands to the "state," and second, to distribute these assets among the New Class.

As Djilas has shown, a New Class regime is a dynamic force, but there is a sharp difference in the way this dyna-

mism has manifested itself in the countries of Eastern
Europe and in Italy. In the former, the New Class was installed at the top by force and in a single stroke at the end
of World War II; its further task has mainly been defensive,
i.e., maintaining its privileged position. In Italy, the starting point at the end of the war was a clean slate: the New
Class had to gain and then to maintain its power, a much
more complicated process which required, in turn, a different strategy, based on a continuous play of alliances and
cooptations.

The Process of Nationalization

The process has been going on since the end of the
[Second World] War, beginning slowly with the first timid
attempts at postwar planning and "welfarization" and then
accelerating dramatically with the opportunities offered in
the late fifties by the Italian "economic miracle." But the
real inauguration of the New Class occurred with the "opening to the Left" of 1961 (carried out with the blessing of the
Kennedy Administration), when the Socialist party was allowed into the government for the first time and a full-
fledged client system was initiated, with all bureaucratic and
paragovernmental positions, down to the last errand boy,
being shared among parties. This was followed by national-
izations and state acquisitions of private industry during the
sixties, as well as by the government's absorption of the
whole Italian financial and banking system. And in the
meantime, of course, government itself was growing: in
1970 alone, the creation of twenty regional authorities, each
with its own miniature parliament, caused an instantaneous
doubling of the bureaucratic structure.

Throughout this entire course of development the numbers and the power of the New Class have increased apace.
The years between 1966 and 1974 saw the takeover, both by
Communists and by clients of the government parties, of
positions in the nationalized industries, banking, the national executive structure, and the school system. The Communist assumption of power at the local level is as much a

symptom as a cause of New Class influence in government, as are the increasing transference of sections of the press to Communist control and the allotment to the Communists of vital positions in parliament. Through its control of the unions and its ability to influence the enactment of laws favorable to its interests, the New Class has overseen the progressive regimentation of the Italian economy, a process which has driven private industry to the wall and brought about the ceding of its assets to the state. Italy is now a country where, by law, workers cannot be discharged even if their employer is going bankrupt; where, also by law, workers are entitled not to work, that is, are entitled to abstain from work for "health reasons" which legally cannot be verified; and where, through the deliberate absence of a law regulating strikes, a firm can be ruined or blackmailed at any time by wildcat strikes.

Cultural Control

Hand in hand with regimentation of the economy has gone New Class dominance of the culture, in particular of the communications media. Here a central role has been played by RAI-TV, a mammoth state monopoly that employs more people and spends more money, in proportion to its output, than any of the American networks, yet keeps the Italian public on a diet of programs as poor and uninformative as they are pretentious. RAI-TV has provided the New Class with its most powerful weapon—the tremendous impact of television propaganda in a not overly literate country—and with its most splendid set of material rewards. Officially, openly, without any pretense of managerial efficiency, RAI-TV distributes millions of dollars' worth of jobs and salaries through a laborious alchemy meant to reflect the vicissitudes of political life. No reference is made to professional competence in the selection process, and every so often a "crisis" of reorganization and expansion is brought about in order to accommodate the perpetually growing ranks of the New Class. . . .

Through RAI-TV, a large portion of the Italian "intellectual" class—above all journalists, but also writers and artists—has been brought out. And thanks to RAI-TV's monopoly over video information, the Italian public has been given a distorted and sometimes brutally falsified picture of the outside world, tailored to the interests and preferences of the New Class. A consistent anti-American slant is only one of the effects; for years the "cultural" programs of RAI-TV have been used to create and reinforce a left-wing image of culture, until today the terms *Left* and *culture* in Italy have become almost synonymous.

Even outside the realm of radio and TV, cultural conformism is the order of the day. New Class dominance of the culture means that only slight and highly circumscribed forms of dissent are tolerated: otherwise one risks ostracism in all cultural fields and complete exclusion from some, like the movies and theater, where the Communists dominate. This development has been facilitated by the hegemony granted by the government to the Communists in the universities and in the school system—Communist activists have been installed as teachers at all levels, and many textbooks even in the elementary grades read like Marxist treatises. Cultural conformism is further facilitated—not just in education but in the whole field of art and culture—by the control over financing exercised by the Communists at the local level. Grade schools are largely financed by local money, and it is also local money that provides most of the funding for the innumerable prizes, art commissions, and scholarships that the New Class distributes among its own. Literary prizes carrying substantial awards number in the hundreds, and ancient Italian piazzas bristle with the officially-commissioned artistic creations of the Italian avant-garde; meanwhile, the Italian government hasn't enough money to keep the museums open even during the tourist season or to protect classic Italian works of art from theft and disfigurement.

In addition to radio and television, the printed press too serves the interests of the New Class. All newspapers have been made completely dependent on the government, which has gradually placed under control every major element in the life of a newspaper: the newsstand price, the supply of printing paper, the allotment of advertising. Newspaper after newspaper has been driven to accumulate enormous deficits, and at the same time has been prevented by the unions from closing; control of the paper then passes directly to the New Class through the various government agencies or through government stand-ins. One such stand-in has been the publisher and industrialist Rizzoli, himself on the verge of bankruptcy, whose firm was summoned to buy out some of the major dailies and transform them into a *presse de régime* [government press]. The deal was closed thanks to an unprecedented loan of $250 million granted to Rizzoli by the state financial agency, IMI, without any visible collateral. Among Rizzoli's ventures has been the purchase of the largest and most influential Italian newspaper, Milan's *Il Corriere della sera,* previously a conservative bulwark of the Italian bourgeoisie, now a covert supporter of Communist entry into the government and, after RAI-TV, the most important vehicle of New Class propaganda in Italy.

The Private Sector

The example of Rizzoli illustrates one interesting feature of the progress of communism in Italy and of the formation of the New Class: the voluntary help given by business, in a way exactly parallel to the course followed during the rise of fascism. Business has found that there are rewards to be had in growing government intervention, and while sometimes it has resisted, at other times it has promptly accepted the system of subsidies and corruption enacted by the New Class.

But whatever the role played by the private business community in bringing about the current state of affairs, in the end none of it would have been possible without the Communist party. A large majority of all laws approved by parliament in the last ten years came about as a result of negotiation with the Communist party. The Communists, furthermore, have systematically used the unions to destabilize the economy. Unceasing pressure by the Communist-controlled unions (usually helped by the smaller but even more aggressive and disruptive unions originally set up by the government parties) has been fundamental in wearing down the private sector. Thus, contrary to the conventional analysis, it is not the dislocation of the Italian economy which has produced the need to give the Communists a new role in government; it is, rather, the role already granted the Communists by the Italian Left which caused the dislocation of the economy.

The Working Class

It is also true that the economic situation has now reached a breaking point that threatens both the Communists and the government, and the New Class that they have created. The "working class" has become restless and unpredictable: the portion that has not joined the New Class in the growing structures of the corporate state has been left out in the cold, and its demands, after having been wildly encouraged, have now become unsatisfiable, except through the short-term and self-defeating remedy of inflationary money printing. Another cause of worry is the "non-working" class, i.e., the vast army of unemployed that has always been a feature of the Italian south. No reliable statistics exist, but in certain areas, like the city of Naples, most of the adult population is perennially unemployed. Until now, all these people have formed the electoral strength of the Communists, but this could change. Both the Communists and their allies in the government run the risk of losing their backing: with the economy at a standstill, something has to give, and the real issue is whether it is to be the parasitic superstructure represented by the New Class, or the standard of life of the rest of the population.

The surfacing of the Communist party at the government level is meant to provide a solution. The Communists have already promised to rein in, through the unions, the very same social class that they themselves, through the same unions, unleashed against the economy. Should that rein-ing-in prove to be unachievable through persuasion, the party could—once it was in power—undoubtedly find other means to force upon the workers the sort of discipline workers already enjoy in Poland and Rumania.

Faced with the prospect of the formal entry of the Communists into the national government, some observers have spoken hopefully of a "communism Italian-style," meaning a regime that would be blander and enjoy a larger consensus than any of those ruling Eastern Europe. It is true that Italians remain Italians, and that the Marxist-Leninist faith of Communist Italians is hardly of the Stalinist or iron type, just as their nationalist-imperialist faith was not of the iron type under fascism. One cannot believe, for example, that in a Communist Italy great masses of political opponents would be exterminated or sent to concentration camps: it is not the Italian style. In fact, this ideological blandness or genial sloppiness is a point Italian Communists proudly make about themselves, and use to political advantage. Nevertheless, it is certain that, once in power, the Communists would retain enough orthodoxy to insure the safety and security of their own power and that of the New Class, of which they would become the guarantors; and it is also certain that under their tutelage the corrupt, nepotistic aristocracy that has been formed in Italy would settle down to its final and undisturbed reward.

ESTABLISHMENT COMMUNISTS? [4]

The students and young workers descended on Bologna twenty thousand strong. Most were dressed in faded jeans, and T shirts or windbreakers; some had daubed their faces with paint, imitating American Indians on the warpath. They surged through the graceful colonnaded streets into the vast Piazza Maggiore for a first skirmish with their

[4] Article entitled "Big Brawl in Bologna: A Leftist Rebuke to Eurocommunism." *Time*. 110:47–8. O. 3, '77. Reprinted by permission from *Time*, the weekly newsmagazine; Copyright Time Inc. 1977.

avowed enemy: the Italian Communist Party (PCI). As the throngs approached Bologna's huge Renaissance-style city hall, a handful of middle-aged Communist apparatchiks [party functionaries] emerged to confront them. "We have been fighting to change things in Italy since 1944," a party militant told a bearded young demonstrator. "What other policy would you have us follow?" The student's quick answer: "A Communist policy." Said another young ultra: "You've given up fighting to change the system, you only want to save it. That's why you're trying to isolate us."

Thus began an improbable three-day conflict between youthful extremists who regard themselves as Marx's true heirs and Europe's largest and most innovative Communist party. The ultras had come to Bologna from all over Italy for a weekend convention held to protest Communist "repression." They claim that the Communist party, in its eagerness to share power with the Christian Democrats, has become a pillar of the Establishment and hates them for saying so.

Specifically, the demonstrators suspect Bologna party leaders, who have proudly and smoothly ruled that city for thirty-two years, of conspiring with the police in the arrest of one hundred student leaders last March [1977]. The trouble began when an auxiliary policeman killed a student who had joined in a Leftist attack on a moderate Catholic group. The boy's death sent thousands of students out of overcrowded Bologna University, whose sixty thousand volatile undergraduates face a bleak future in Italy's recession-bound economy. For three days, the students occupied a twenty-block commercial area, manhandling citizens, looting stores and burning cars in an orgy of youthful anarchism that was unprecedented, even in Italy.

The riots were deeply mortifying to the Communists, especially since they took place in Bologna, which the party has always pointed to as a paradigm of how it would work within a pluralistic society. Stung by the protests, Bologna party leaders suspected Italy's secret service, the

CIA or other foreign intelligence outfits of manipulating extremists in order to discredit the Communists. Party leaders are especially bitter about a Parisian manifesto signed by twenty-six Leftist intellectuals, including writer Jean-Paul Sartre, accusing the Italian party of brutally putting down the students in Bologna.

The PCI held a mass conclave in Modena on the eve of . . . [the September 1977] demonstrations in Bologna. "Let these youths carry their insults against our party," declared Party Chief Enrico Berlinguer. "Bologna will surely not be disrupted by their lies." Berlinguer accused them of regarding "the Communist party as the enemy to be defeated. In a bitter reference to the French intellectuals' manifesto, he noted that "the Right wing often disguises itself as Leftist, and cultural idiots at home and abroad fall right into the trap."

The young ultras are far better at saying what they are against than what they are for. They tend to be naive about economics, innocent of history and full of fragmentary utopian ideas. On the first day of their conclave, twelve thousand youths from a dozen factions jammed the Palasport, Bologna's main sports arena, for a four-hour meeting that was billed as a debate but was more like a shouting match. The crowd cheered one self-styled "comrade from Milan" who complained of Communist persecution of independent Leftists in his factory. Another speaker concluded: "What we need now is organization. We've already shown we can fight." Already deeply impressed by the demonstrators' fighting capacity, the Italian parliament is considering a series of tough new bills designed to curb terrorism and rioting.

VI. THE SUPERPOWERS: DÉTENTE AND DEFENSE

EDITOR'S INTRODUCTION

In this concluding section, the developments of national communism are placed in the context of their effect on the policies of the so-called superpowers. This shift in perspective introduces parallel problems at different levels of analysis. The problems that face individual nations—autonomy, revolution, and assistance—become, at the level of the superpowers, problems of détente, control, and defense.

The opening article, by Professor Alvin Z. Rubinstein of the University of Pennsylvania, can be taken as a text for analyzing the speeches of the American and Soviet heads of state that are reprinted in this section. Rubinstein traces three post–World War II trends—national communism, Eurocommunism, and Finlandization (a form of submissive neutrality)—in terms of the problems they pose for Soviet objectives in Europe.

The address of Leonid Brezhnev, general secretary of the Communist Party of the Soviet Union, at the much-discussed 1976 Pan-European Communist parties conference—of which the final third is reprinted here—outlines his concerns and is significant for the terms he uses in an appeal for unity: the denial that "calls to strengthen international bonds uniting the Communists signify a desire to recreate some organizational center"; a concern with the military threat posed by NATO; affirmation of the value and role of Eurocommunists in a common revolutionary endeavor.

There is a convergence between Brezhnev's hopes and former Secretary of State Henry A. Kissinger's fears, which are expressed in the next selection, a critique from the

New York *Times* of the Carter Administration's attitude toward Eurocommunism. Carter's later shift in position is shown in the fourth article and in the fifth and final selection, the President's March 17, 1978, address on defense and Soviet ties.

Delivered to protest Soviet intervention in Africa, this last-mentioned speech is a review of changes and diversity in the Communist world that make Cold War labels inapplicable. It too places hope in détente, cooperation, and disarmament. But it is concerned with a posture of defense, military coalition, and assistance to prevent large blocs of the world in Europe, Africa, and Asia from falling under the domination of a single power. Like Brezhnev's address, like other statements in this volume, like the history of national Communist parties and their international alliances, it reflects a continuing dilemma.

SOVIET POLICY IN EUROPE [1]

Europe holds the key to the future of the Soviet Union and the United States. Each superpower seeks to encourage the evolution of its own kind of Europe, and many cold war tensions are generated over these competing conceptions. With all the attention being given détente, SALT [Strategic Arms Limitation Treaty], trade, technological transfers, competition in Southern and Eastern Africa—most of which relates primarily to the Soviet-American relationship—there is a tendency to forget that the cold war began in Europe; moreover, it is in Europe that the stakes in the Soviet-American rivalry are the greatest. Thus, even though the nations of Europe no longer play a vital international role, they have a significant effect on the long-range policies and outlooks of the superpowers.

The expansion of Soviet power into the center of Europe

[1] From an article by Alvin Z. Rubinstein, professor of political science at the University of Pennsylvania, author of numerous books on the USSR, editor of *Soviet and Chinese Influence in the Third World* (Praeger, 1975). *Current History.* 73:105–8+. O. '77. Copyright © 1977 by Current History, Inc. Reprinted by permission.

is the most important consequence of World War II. In analyzing Soviet policy toward East and West Europe, the Soviet Union's nuclear and missile capability and its enormous buildup of conventional forces must be remembered; and the Western powers must stay alert to the ever-present military threat posed by Soviet power. But beyond that there are underlying forces of complexity and intensity that defy easy explanation and complicate the formulation of foreign policy for both Soviet leaders and their counterparts in the West.

Soviet foreign policy gives pride of place to Europe. The Soviet Union consistently devotes more attention to developments in Europe than in any other region of the world. Not even China holds the same importance. Accordingly, it may be useful to examine the evolution of Soviet policy towards Europe, both East and West.

Three broad trends—national communism, Finlandization, and Eurocommunism—have given rise to distinctive developments, each of which has created new challenges for the Soviet leadership.

National Communism

The term *national communism* refers to a fusion of nationalism and communism in a political outlook and movement with a variety of forms, which seeks greater independence from Soviet military and ideological domination. In the context of East Europe, national communism has three times given rise to a quest for autonomy unacceptable to Moscow: in Yugoslavia in 1948, in Hungary in 1956, and in Czechoslovakia in 1968. No single explanation can fully explain national communism, which must be viewed in specific frameworks of historical and political circumstances.

National communism was an unanticipated consequence of Soviet domination. At the end of World War II, with the defeat of Nazi Germany, the Soviet Union occupied Poland, Czechoslovakia, Hungary, Rumania, Bulgaria and East Germany, installed pro-Moscow Communist parties in power, imposed Stalinist modes of government, and exploited these countries economically in order to rebuild its own devastated economy. . . . The presence of the Red army in the center of Europe led West Europe to fear further Soviet expansion. This concern led to the formation of the North Atlantic Treaty Organization (NATO) in 1949 and the subsequent remilitarization of the United States, especially after the Korean War.

By the time Joseph Stalin died in March 1953, Europe had been polarized along political-ideological lines, and the Soviet imperium was unchallenged in the areas occupied by the Red army. Yugoslavia and Albania had escaped a Soviet "liberation" in 1945, and as a result their indigenous Communist parties ruled free of Moscow's dictate. Although he was a disciple of Stalin's and the most truculently anti-Western of all the East European Communists, Yugoslav President Tito refused to turn Yugoslavia into a slavish satrapy of the Soviet Union, insisting instead that the Yugoslav Communist party be allowed to run its own show. Stalin tried to topple Tito by excommunicating Yugoslavia from the Soviet bloc in June 1948, but this ploy failed and "national communism" (originally called "Titoism") was born. Moscow then adopted harsh measures to expunge the Titoist heresy from East Europe and preserve its own unquestioned authority as leader of the world Communist movement.

A number of developments forced Stalin's successors to moderate the crude and exploitative aspects of Soviet rule over East Europe. The struggle for power within the Soviet hierarchy prompted far-reaching policies to discard outmoded aspects of the Stalinist model of rule. Soviet leaders wanted to establish relations with their East European empire on a sounder and more efficient economic basis, while ensuring the political-military cohesion of the bloc. Soviet leaders also hoped to restore comradely relations with Yugoslavia. They began to emphasize "peaceful coexistence" with the West, trying to prevent West Germany's rearmament and integration into NATO and to encourage a withdrawal of American power from Europe. Growing frictions with Communist China also enhanced the need for a secure and reliable East Europe.

Inexorably, de-Stalinization led to differentiation and diversity. Moscow's power remained preeminent, but Soviet proposals were no longer unquestioningly accepted. Seeking to rule through consensus rather than coercion, the Soviet leadership found itself thwarted by East Europe's innate suspicion of Soviet intentions and the East European desire for increased autonomy. Soviet Premier Nikita Khrushchev, for example, sought to promote economic integration and planning for Soviet bloc members through the Council for Mutual Economic Assistance (COMECON). He wanted to establish a "socialist international division of labor," in which each country in East Europe would specialize in certain commodities, in order to increase efficiency and reduce costs to COMECON members. But Khrushchev's economically rational proposal encountered considerable opposition from the Rumanians and the Poles, in large part because they feared that economic integration would jeopardize their newly acquired autonomy and would bring them again under total Soviet authority. Thus, although there are sound economic reasons for promoting bloc integration, and although a few joint projects, like the DRUZHBA natural gas line, have been completed, memories of the Stalin period and residual distrust of Moscow engender a continuing resistance. Furthermore, Moscow has tolerated, and on occasions even encouraged, the expansion of East European economic ties with the nations of West Europe, which has offered substantial credit for industrial purchases in the West. In this way, Moscow hopes the bloc will modernize its economies and become more of an economic asset.

Since May 1955, the Soviet military presence in East Europe has been legitimized by the Warsaw Pact. Soviet leaders used their power in Hungary in 1956 and in Czechoslovakia in 1968 to suppress what they regarded as threats to the Communist and Soviet-dominated character of the area. Thus, with an iron hand inside a velvet glove, the Soviet Union has kept the East Europeans in line. Rumania, for example, has been careful not to exceed the political parameters tolerated by Moscow. In a number of ways Rumania has acted very much the maverick: developing friendly relations with Peking in the face of deteriorating Soviet relations with China; maintaining diplomatic and economic relations with Israel despite Moscow's contrary policy since June 1967; encouraging large-scale Western (especially West German) investment while resisting integration within COMECON; refusing to participate in the Soviet-engineered invasion of Czechoslovakia in 1968 by Warsaw Pact forces. But always, Rumania's leadership has avoided provoking the Soviet leadership with internal liberalization or a direct challenge to Moscow's position in East Europe. The "Brezhnev Doctrine"—Moscow's assertion of its right to intervene anywhere in the "Socialist" world to preserve "socialism"—has forced Rumania and other bloc members to be careful not to overstep the bounds of autonomy set by Moscow.

Yet Soviet needs, bloc pressures, and changes in the European environment and the international Communist movement require that Moscow constantly recalibrate the limits of East Europe's autonomy. Soviet military power in East Europe has never been greater, but Moscow finds its authority increasingly challenged and it faces its policy dilemmas with growing uneasiness. Can the Soviet Union continue to dole out bits of autonomy to satisfy pent-up nationalist desires without eroding the stability and cohesiveness of its "security community" in East Europe? How far can it go in encouraging economic ties between East and West Europe without relinquishing its own ambitions to form a viable economic community and without forcing a revamping of its own economic institutions and practices? At what point is national communism apt to become more national than Communist and therefore more anti-Soviet and more difficult to manage within a Moscow-controlled system?

Finlandization

With due apologies to the Finns, we use the term *Finlandization*, which has come to signify a process whereby the Soviet Union influences the domestic and foreign-policy behavior of non-Communist countries in a way that leads them to follow policies congenial to, or approved by, the Soviet Union. The long-term Soviet objective is to dominate West Europe without having to use force. One British specialist puts the matter succinctly:

The Russians would like Western Europe to be made up of militarily weak nation-states, each spending very little on defense, and joined by no effective military alliance; they would like an end to the American military presence in Europe and the Mediterranean, and to existing American guarantees to West European defence. They would like economic rivalry to replace cooperation, and an end to prospects of West European political cohesion or future integration. (Malcolm MacKintosh, "Future Soviet Policy Towards Western Europe," *in* John C. Garnett, ed. *The Defence of Western Europe*. Macmillan, 1974, p 44.)

As always, however, reality is more complex than the theories or conceptual formulations that seek to explain it. West Europe remains independent and NATO is still the keystone of the West European and United States security community. Economic integration and cooperation among the West European countries have progressed somewhat, though not nearly so much as its partisans had hoped. United States military commitments to the defense of West Europe seem secure; and the basic policies of the West European countries appear to be more a function of their domestic politics and interallied bargaining and bickering than of Soviet influence.

The West's disarray, which Moscow naturally tries to exploit, cannot be attributed to the Soviet Union. George F. Kennan, among others, has argued that the "Finlandization" of the West, if it should come to pass, would be the consequence of Western weakness, not Soviet strength. In his judgment, Soviet leaders are "not inclined towards major innovations of policy, particularly not risky or adventurous ones":

> They [Soviet leaders] face many serious internal problems, and their whole motivation in external relations is basically defensive: defensive against the Chinese political attack, defensive against the disturbing implications of continued Western economic and technological superiority. It is absurd to picture these men as embarked on some new and dark plot to achieve the subjugation of, and the domination over, Western Europe. They are committed, to be sure, to a whole series of habitual postures, reactions, and rhetorical utterances that may appear to bear in that direction. But none of these manifestations of Soviet behavior are new; none are inspired by any belief in the possibility of their early success; and there are none that should be occasioning for Western statesmen any greater anxieties than they were experiencing—say—ten or fifteen years ago before détente ever began to be talked about. . . .
>
> Poor old West: succumbing feebly, day by day, to its own decadence, sliding into debility on the slime of its own self-indulgent permissiveness: its drugs, its crime, its pornography, its pampering of the youth, its addiction to its bodily comforts, its rampant materialism and consumerism—and then trembling before the menace of the wicked Russians, all pictured as supermen, eight feet tall, their internal problems all essentially solved, and with nothing else now to think about except how to bring damage and destruction to Western Europe. This persistent externalization of the sense of danger . . . and blindness to the threat from within . . . is the symptom of some deep failure to come to terms with reality—and with one's self. If Western Europe could bring itself to think a little less about how defenseless it is in the face of the Russians, and a little more about what it is that it has to defend, I would feel more comfortable about its prospects for the future. (George F. Kennan, "Are All Russians 8 Feet Tall . . . And Is the West Blind to the Threat from Within?" *Freedom at Issue*, September-October 1976, p 16.)

. . . But those who take a far less optimistic view of Soviet intentions in Europe maintain that the underestimation of Moscow's threat and of its multifaceted diplomacy, which seeks to undermine the West's will to resist, tends to discount important developments. Two may be cited. The chilling momentum underlying the Soviet military buildup of conventional forces in Europe has created an ominous imbalance between the Warsaw Pact and NATO: today the theater warfare capability of Soviet infantry, tank corps, artillery, and logistical systems have all been greatly expanded and modernized.

In addition, the Soviet Union gained a notable diplomatic triumph with the convening in Helsinki of the Conference on Security and Cooperation in Europe (CSCE) and the signing of the Final Act of the CSCE on August 1, 1975. Moscow first proposed such a conference in 1954; its aims were Western recognition of the territorial division of Europe along post-1945 lines; international recognition of the East German regime; and acceptance of the Soviet sphere of influence in East Europe. These objectives were realized in 1975.

The critics of Helsinki contend that the agreement made Soviet borrowing from West European governments and firms easier, lowered the barriers to Soviet importation of much-needed advanced technology, gave Moscow additional leverage for playing off one Western country against another, and nurtured acceptance in the West of the permanence of Soviet power in the center of Europe.

Western defenders of the Final Act insist that Moscow paid a price for its gains. The Soviet Union agreed to honor the principle of peaceful settlement of disputes, nonintervention in the domestic affairs of other states, and cooperation in humanitarian and cultural fields, including the freer movement of people and information, family reunification and visits, and educational exchanges—the so-called Basket Three provisions. If implemented, these principles would reduce tensions and would further perforate the Iron Curtain that has divided Europe for so many years.

As a result of the Helsinki accords, the USSR has also agreed to give prior notice of large-scale troop maneuvers. This "confidence-building" measure is a step in the direction of easing tensions. The manifestations of dissidence in Poland and Czechoslovakia and to some extent even in Rumania and East Germany suggest that Basket Three provisions could become a problem for Moscow, further complicating its exercise of authority over a restive East Europe. Soviet concern can be seen in its vehement attacks on the "imperialist circles" that lead the campaign for human rights and in its attempts to fashion a unified bloc position at the June 1977 meeting in Belgrade preparatory to the formal conference. . . .

The record of Soviet efforts to Finlandize West Europe remains to be written. The Soviet leaders face several dilemmas. How far can they reduce tensions and thereby encourage a reduced United States military presence in Europe without occasioning intolerable demands for autonomy from their East European client states? Would a weak and dependent West Europe lobby for a greater United States presence, which Moscow seeks to forestall? Can Moscow exploit nationalism and national animosities in the West and, at the same time, nurture integration and regional cooperation in East Europe? If Moscow uses its muscle to change West European policies, as for example in trying to prevent the organizers of Italy's prestigious Venice Biennale from exhibiting the works of East European dissident artists, or proscribing West European contacts with Soviet dissidents, may it not reinforce the position of partisans of a stronger NATO, who will cite such interference as a harbinger of things to come?

Eurocommunism

The phenomenon of Eurocommunism, about which so much is being written nowadays, refers to the entry of West European Communist parties into the political mainstreams of their respective countries and their professed commitment to an evolutionary quest for power and a readiness to share office in coalition with non-Communist parties. . . . Eurocommunism may be considered to have taken shape in mid-November 1975 with the manifesto issued in Rome by the Italian Communist leader Enrico Berlinguer and his French counterpart, Georges Marchais, in which they gave their support "for the plurality of political parties, for the right to existence and activity of opposition parties, and for democratic alternation between the majority and the minority." (Kevin Devlin, "The Challenge of Eurocommunism," *Problems of Communism*, January-February 1977, p 9.)

Santiago Carrillo, general secretary of the recently legalized Spanish Communist party, has been the most outspoken in staking out a maverick position on the relationship between a West European Communist party and the Soviet Union. In an interview in February 1976 with the Milan newspaper *Corriere della sera*, he declared himself not worried at the prospect of Soviet condemnation of heretical centers of communism: "By what right could they condemn us? They can criticize us, as we criticize them. Condemnation is excommunication from a church, and the Communist movement was a church but now no longer is one."

On another occasion, the Spanish Communist equated democracy with Western democracy and "not a people's democracy as in Eastern Europe"; furthermore, he said: "I mistrust the Russians as much as you do. We have to keep United States bases in Spain for a while. Certainly, as long as Russia has bases in Czechoslovakia, the U.S.A. should have bases in Spain." (New York *Times*, April 23, 1977.)

What all this means for Soviet foreign policy is far from clear. Moscow has no way of exercising direct control over any West European Communist party. It must tolerate criticism and try through persuasion to fashion a consensus that leaves Soviet leadership more or less intact in the international Communist movement—especially in East Europe.

Moscow has been unable to gain unquestioned acceptance of its ideological and political preeminence. In 1974 and 1975, it failed to win over key leaderships of European Communist parties. The Yugoslavs, the Rumanians, the Italians and the French, among others, were unwilling to accept the "leading" position of the Soviet party and insisted on equality for all parties. At the twenty-fifth Congress of the Communist party of the Soviet Union in March

1976, Soviet Party Secretary Leonid Brezhnev hoped for agreement to the principle of "proletarian international-ism" (the euphemism for Moscow's leadership), but he backed down in the face of widespread opposition. And at the Conference of European Communist Parties, held in East Berlin on June 29 and 30, 1976—the first such inter-national gathering that Yugoslav President Tito attended since Stalin excommunicated him from the Cominform in June 1948—the Soviets had to accept a document that said "there is no leading center of international communism."

Polemics and political opportunism aside, Soviet leaders can take comfort from the general support they receive from West European Communists on most foreign policy issues. In the long run, this may be the most important as-pect of Eurocommunism for the Soviet leadership.

In the short term, Eurocommunism is far more a chal-lenge for the West than for the Soviet Union. If a NATO country were to go Communist, could it remain in an alli-ance created as a defense against the Soviet Union? Can Communists be trusted with military secrets? Will the Com-munists, once they are in power, behave according to the rules of democratic politics?

Yet Eurocommunism also poses serious problems for Moscow. While the rising electoral popularity of West Euro-pean Communist parties may weaken the position of the bourgeois anti-Soviet opposition, what can Moscow do to prevent the virus of Communist diversity from spreading to East Europe? Would the success of West European Communist parties encourage East Europeans to demand greater autonomy, thereby weakening the Soviet grip on its Warsaw Pact members? Is diversity a prelude to the disin-tegration of Moscow's hitherto dominant position in East Europe? Is there a spillover effect from West European com-munism to East European communism?

Observations

For the moment, no major crisis faces the Soviet leader-ship. However, the Kremlin's policy of drift and the relative tolerance of the last decade may not be adequate for the 1980s. The Soviet Union faces an aging leadership, an economy in chronic difficulty and a growing gap between the Soviet bloc and the West in many areas of technology. In a restive East Europe, human rights activists are surfacing to bedevil the anxious authoritarians in the party hierarchies. A point of no return may be approaching in the strategic arms relationship between the Soviet Union and the United States. Thus the Kremlin may soon have to come to grips with the new realities that are emerging in a changing Europe. Power alone will not be an adequate substitute for a coherent policy. The challenge goes to the very heart of Moscow's imperial position.

BREZHNEV'S COMMON CAUSE [2]

Dear Comrades, The delegation of the Communist party of the Soviet Union warmly greets the participants in this conference of Communist and workers' parties of Europe. We convey to you the feelings of brotherly friendship and militant solidarity from the 15.5 million Soviet Communists. We also cordially thank our comrades from the Socialist Unity party of Germany and personally Comrade Honecker for their attention, for the excellent organization of our conference.

Present in this hall are the leading figures of twenty-nine Communist parties of Europe. Gathered here are people who devoted their life to the struggle for the rights of working people; for a new, just social order; for a really lasting peace among peoples. Our parties work under different conditions and tackle various tasks, shaping their tactics and strategy according to the concrete situation in their respective countries. But all of us are participants in a

[2] From an address entitled "The European Communist Parties: The Communists Remain Revolutionaries," by Leonid Brezhnev, general secretary of the Communist party of the Soviet Union, delivered at the Conference of European Communist and Workers' Parties, East Berlin, German Democratic Republic, June 29, 1976. Vital Speeches of the Day. 42:610–16. Ag. 1, '76. Reprinted by permission.

single struggle, all of us are moving in the same direction and all of us are united by a common, noble ultimate goal. This is why for us European Communists it is useful, in the interests of our common cause, to exchange views and discuss such important and topical themes as peace, cooperation, security and social progress in Europe.

It may be considered in a certain measure symbolic that we have gathered here in Berlin—a city where Hitlerism was finally routed, a city which only thirty years ago lay in ruins, a city which today offers a splendid example of revival, flourishing and of aspiration to advance. Today this is the capital of the German Democratic Republic, a state whose designs are connected, as was recently confirmed once again by the 9th Congress of the SUPG [Socialist Unity Party of Germany], with peaceful creative labor in the name of a Communist future.

And now this Berlin hospitably receives the Communists of Europe, convened to offer her peoples the roads for advancing to new horizons of peace and social progress. Here, indeed, is a striking indicator of the historic changes in Europe. . . .

Today's achievements of the peoples of Europe are, above all, the result of the liberation struggle against the Fascist aggressors and enslavers.

Today's Europe is in considerable measure the result of the successful building of socialism and communism in a number of the continent's countries. It is also the result of the persistent and unwavering struggle for peace waged in the countries of socialism on the international scene.

At the same time, Europe's new face is the result of the mounting class struggles by working people in bourgeois countries led by the working class, the result of struggles in broad public circles for a lasting peace.

An important distinctive feature of the period we are living through is that these changes are taking place in today's Europe against a background of the deepening general crisis of capitalism, . . . [not] only an economic crisis but a political and moral crisis as well. It convinces the masses even more that capitalism is a society without a future, thereby multiplying the number of supporters of the other, Socialist way. This crisis cannot be arrested either by shoring up imperialist military-political blocs and the arms race, or by economic integration of monopolies, the semblance of social reforms, or repressions. . . .

Disarmament: Détente and NATO

In the new conditions that appeared in Europe, many acute and explosive problems that had convulsed the continent since the Second World War, have at long last found a solution. Important treaties and agreements concluded in recent years by the Socialist states with France, the FRG [Federal Republic of Germany] and other Western countries, and the Quadripartite agreement on West Berlin have changed the international situation in Europe for the better. [The Quadripartite agreement on access to West Berlin was signed in 1971 by the United States, Britain, France, and the Soviet Union.—Ed.]

The principles of peaceful coexistence have become the leading tendency in relations between states. This found its fullest expression in the success of the European Conference with the participation of the United States and Canada. . . .

It demonstrated how justified were the stands taken by realistically-minded representatives of the ruling circles in the bourgeois countries. Yet it also alerted and activated the forces of reaction and militarism. . . . It alarmed all those who grow rich by the manufacture of weapons of death and destruction, those who cannot imagine a political career other than firing up a "crusade" against the countries of socialism, against Communists, or, like the Maoist leaders of China who openly urge to "prepare for a new war," count on profiting by pitting other states and peoples against each other.

The opposition of these diverse forces to relaxation of tension assumes different forms. The main among them, however, is the striving to intensify still more an arms race that has already attained unprecedented scope.

To this end the aggressive forces of imperialism and their stooges again resort to the time-worn myth about the notorious "Soviet menace," . . . [blaming Socialist countries] for civil and national-liberation wars. . . .

But, no sooner does one turn to facts, to reality, than these fabrications collapse like a house of cards.

Speaking of Central Europe, there is no great difference in the size of the armed forces of the Warsaw Treaty member-countries and those of NATO. They exist, and have for many years now, on a more or less equal level. . . .

This is why the Socialist countries propose to agree to an equal reduction of the sides' armed forces and armaments (at least of the USSR and the USA to begin with) so as not to alter the correlation of forces but to reduce the sides' military spending and the risk of a clash. Nothing, it would seem, could be more logical and fair. But no, the NATO countries are stubbornly trying to get an unequal reduction so that the correlation of forces would change to their advantage and to the detriment of the Socialist states. . . .

The Soviet Union is the only great power which does not increase its military spending from year to year and works for a general concerted reduction of the powers' military budgets. Meanwhile the military budget of the USA is growing incessantly. . . . The military spending of NATO's West European member-countries has more than doubled in the five years from 1971 to 1975. . . .

Given present-day conditions, any concrete measures aimed at preserving and strengthening the beginnings of trust that are shaping up in East-West relations are extremely valuable.

The Soviet Union, loyal . . . [to] the Helsinki accords, duly informs the parties to the European Conference about military exercises held in border zones and invites observers from neighboring states to watch them.

As is known, the Socialist countries have repeatedly suggested a simultaneous disbandment of the North Atlantic and the Warsaw Treaty Organizations or, as a preliminary step, the liquidation of their military organizations.

We are, of course, far from the idea of equating the two organizations. The Warsaw Treaty is a purely defensive organization. As to NATO, this bloc was established as an instrument of aggression and of suppression of the liberation struggle of the peoples and it remains such, whatever is done to embellish its activities. But we are against the division of the world into military blocs on principle and are prepared to do everything possible for the two groupings to cease their activities simultaneously. . . .

Economic Cooperation and Détente

Indeed, peace has become a vital necessity for Europe and the Europeans. Therefore we Communists, proponents of the most humanitarian, life-asserting world outlook, believe that it is now more important than ever before to pave the way for the relaxation of military tension and to stop the arms race. It is also extremely important to create, so to speak, the material fabric of peaceful cooperation in Europe; a fabric that would strengthen ties among European peoples and states and would make them more interested in preserving peace for many years to come.

I have in view various forms of mutually beneficial cooperation: trade, cooperation in production, scientific and technical ties.

This is quite a feasible task. In recent years, living in a climate of progressing relaxation of tension, the East and West European states have gained considerable experience of such cooperation. For example, the Soviet Union's trade with the European capitalist countries has more than trebled over the last five years. Cooperation in building large-scale projects on the basis of mutual benefit is assuming ever greater importance.

I think that the European Communists all agree that the further development of such ties is useful and desirable. Such ties help create a material foundation for a lasting peace. They meet the vital interests of the working people. Suffice it to say that according to figures published in the

West, economic ties with the Socialist countries have already provided jobs for hundreds of thousands or even millions of people in Western Europe in this time of crisis. . . .

Cultural Exchange: No Closed Society

Comrades, to create a climate of trust between states that is so needed for a lasting peace, it is necessary for the peoples to come to know and understand each other better. It is primarily from this point of view that we approach the questions of cultural exchanges and human contacts in all their diversity.

What is the state of affairs in this field? We in the Soviet Union consider it important that our people should know more about the past and the present of other peoples, have a deeper knowledge of their culture, and respect the historical experience and achievements of other countries.

Therefore the Soviet Union encourages cultural exchanges in every way. It consolidates them by means of intergovernmental agreements and expands them from year to year. At present our country maintains cultural ties with 120 countries. In accordance with the Final Act of the Helsinki Conference we took additional measures to increase the exchange of books, films and works of art. The other Socialist countries, participants in the European Conference, are known to be following a similar line.

As to the capitalist states, we have heard many fine words from them about the exchange of cultural values but seen few actions.

This is to be seen in different fields. In Britain and France, for instance, they publish six-seven times less books by Soviet authors than we in the Soviet Union publish works by English and French writers. In the Western countries, they show tens of times fewer Soviet films than we show Western films, three times fewer Soviet TV programs, and so on and so forth.

On the whole, the peoples of the Socialist countries are much better informed about life in the West than the working masses in the capitalist countries about life in the

Socialist countries. Why? The deepest of the reasons is that the ruling class in the bourgeois countries does not want the working people in their countries to learn from a first-hand source the truth about the Socialist countries, their social and cultural development, the political and moral principles of citizens in a Socialist society.

To weaken the force of attraction of socialism and to tar its image, bourgeois propaganda has invented a myth about a "closed society." It asserts that the Socialist countries allegedly avoid communicating with other peoples and shrink from exchanging information and developing contacts among people.

Here too let us turn to 1975 facts. Alone, the CMEA [COMECON, the Council for Mutual Economic Assistance, a trade organization of East European Socialist countries] countries were visited by 58 million foreign guests. On the other hand, about 35 million citizens of Socialist countries made trips abroad. This alone clearly shows what all the talk about a "closed society" is worth.

Or take the question of contacts between such mass organizations as trade unions. More than once state organs in the USA denied visas to Soviet trade union delegations that were invited by American trade unions. There have been even cases when they refused to let representatives of Soviet trade unions attend international meetings held in the territory of the USA.

As to the USSR, it was visited last year by 980 foreign trade union and workers' delegations while 750 Soviet delegations went to foreign countries.

Closed to Subversion

No, the Socialist countries are not a "closed society." We are open to everything truthful and honest and we are prepared to multiply contacts by using the favorable conditions offered by the relaxation of tension. But our doors will always be closed to publications that advocate war, violence, racism, and manhating views. All the more so, they will be closed to emissaries of foreign secret services and anti-Soviet emigré organizations created by them. Indeed, in talking about the "freedom" of contacts some people in the West sometimes only think of securing freedom of action for very nasty things. We are not sick with "spy mania." But we shall not give freedom for subversive actions against our system, our society. I think that after the recent scandalous exposures concerning the activities of the US Central Intelligence Agency everyone will see clearly that we have some reasons, to put it mildly, for such an approach to the matter.

We think that cultural exchanges and information media should serve humanitarian ideals, the cause of peace, and the strengthening of trust and friendship between the peoples. Meantime, well-known subversive radio stations which have usurped the names *Liberty* and *Free Europe* are operating in the territories of some European countries. The very existence of such stations poisons the international atmosphere and is a direct challenge to the spirit and letter of the Helsinki accords. The Soviet Union resolutely comes out for the termination of the operation of these instruments of "psychological warfare." . . .

Socialist Prosperity: Productivity, Egalitarianism, Education

The scale of our national economy today is enormous. Suffice it to say that the Soviet Union accounts for 20 percent of the world's industrial output. In absolute figures, this is more than was produced throughout the world in 1950. . . .

The advantages of socialism enable us to ensure the country's continuous economic growth and at the same time a continuous rise in the welfare of the entire people. At present our party puts to the forefront the task of enhancing the efficiency of production and raising the standard of performance in all aspects of this many-faceted concept. This calls for an enormous amount of work to be done in various fields: from a sweeping renovation of the technical basis of production to new serious advances in the work of cultivating a politically conscious, Communist attitude to work;

220 The Reference Shelf

and in developing the initiative of the multimillioned masses of the working people.

I think it important to underline that in developing production and raising the living standards of the people we do not regard this as an end in itself but approach the matter with due account taken of the main program goals of Communist construction.

I have in mind specifically the goal of narrowing the margin of difference between the living conditions of people in town and countryside, which is one of the aims of the agrarian policy that was worked out by our party in recent years. There is also the goal of gradually eradicating the difference between brainwork and manual work, a process which is helped, for instance, by the introduction of universal compulsory ten-year schooling and the rising intellectual level of the work done by workers and collective farmers. By launching housing construction on an unprecedented large scale we have also done much to provide tens of millions of working people with adequate modern housing at a record low rent. . . .

Democratic Participation

The successes of our social development are possible only as a result of free and politically conscious work of the masses, ever more active exercise of their civil rights, and ever more active participation by the masses in shaping all aspects of public life. Therefore, our further advance in building communism will necessarily be accompanied by the further development of Socialist democracy. Such is the principled policy of our party, such is our reality.

Under the conditions of socialism, Soviet man has developed what is truly a valuable quality: a sense of being the master of his country who clearly sees the connection between his work and the cause of the whole nation and who always remembers and thinks of common interests. . . .

If a skilled worker at a factory or in the field attains the best production results and leaves his workmates behind, his concern, as a rule, is to pass on his experience to others, to make it a common possession. There are, perhaps, no people in our society held in greater esteem than front-rankers in production. Many of them are well known throughout the country. The newspapers write about them and they are elected to organs of state power.

Over 2 million working people in our country are invested with this state power and are elected to the Soviets. But this is not all. Almost 30 million Soviet citizens work as activists in the Soviets and help voluntarily, on a non-salaried basis, in the great and complicated work of state administration. Nine million people are working on elected people's control bodies which keep under close watch the work of different sections of management and fight against manifestations of bureaucracy and unconscientious attitude to work.

There is one more form of activity of working people: standing production conferences, of which 65 percent consist of workers, have been established at Soviet enterprises. Over a million proposals worked out by such conferences for improving production and working conditions were carried out .. [in 1975] alone.

These are only some of the many examples but they, I think, give a good idea of how the work of administrative bodies is combined in our country with democracy at the grass-root level.

There are certainly many shortcomings and outstanding problems in our great and complicated social life. But . . . we have built a society free from the dominance of a monopoly oligarchy, a society free from fear of crisis, unemployment, and free from social calamities. We have created a society of people equal in the broadest sense of the word; people who know no social, property, racial or any other privilege: a society which not only proclaims human rights but also actually guarantees the possibility of exercising them. We have created a society that is stable, dynamic and united.

It can be said with certainty, comrades, that never before have the working people of our country enjoyed such high

living standards as today. Never before have they had such a
high education level and such opportunities of enjoying
cultural values as now. Never before have they felt as confident of tomorrow, of a peaceful future, or of their country,
as today. That is the basis of the Soviet people's unanimous
support for the . . . policy [of the Communist Party of the
Soviet Union], the basis of the unbreakable unity of the
party and the people in our country.

The International Movement: Comrades in Capitalist Countries

Comrades, the development of events in the world is
increasingly determined by the anti-imperialist forces which
are opposed to oppression and exploitation, to violence and
arbitrariness in international affairs. A great deal depends
on the cohesion of these forces and their interaction.

The fraternal solidarity of the Socialist countries adds to
the might of each of them; economic cooperation on an
equal footing adds tremendous potentialities to its own
resources. The profound, organic and ever-growing friendly
ties between party and state organs, between the labor col-
lectives of factories and scientific institutions and public
organizations, between millions and millions of citizens give
us ground to speak of an absolutely new phenomenon: a
truly fraternal union of peoples that have commonly held
views and goals. The comradeship-in-arms of the Marxist-
Leninist parties constitutes the strong foundation of this
union, its cementing force.

Interaction between the Communists of the Socialist and
capitalist countries is playing a tremendously important
role. Nine years ago, representatives of many fraternal parties in both parts of our continent together drew up a
program of struggle for peace and security in Europe. Now
everybody can see that this program has in the main been
translated into reality.

We, Soviet Communists, just as Communists in other
Socialist countries, are deeply grateful to our comrades from
the capitalist countries who solidarized with us both at diffi-

cult moments in our history and in the days of normal peaceful work. We, for our part, always solidarize with the struggle waged by our class brothers in the camp of capitalism and strive to give them moral and political support.

The vigorous activity of the Communists in the countries of Western Europe, their perseverance in the struggle for the masses, for uniting the working class and all the forces capable of struggle against the power of the monopolies, for the establishment of truly democratic regimes, for creating prerequisites for the transition to socialism, are bearing fruit. It is thanks to the consistent and tireless struggle for the vital interests of the broad popular masses that the Communist parties of Italy and France, Finland and Portugal, and also of Denmark, the Federal Republic of Germany, and other capitalist countries have turned into important political forces. Some of the convincing testimonies of this was the outstanding success of the Italian Communist party in the recent parliamentary elections, a success in which we all rejoice and on which we congratulate our Italian comrades.

It is of special importance that, when uniting in the struggle against reactionary imperialist circles with broad democratic streams, including Social Democrats and Christians, the Communists remain revolutionaries, convinced champions of replacing the capitalist system by a Socialist one. It is to the solution of this historical task that they subordinate all their activities.

No Organizational Center

Every Communist party is born of the working-class movement of the country in which it is active. And it is responsible for its actions first of all before the working people of its own country whose interests it expresses and defends. But it is precisely this that provides the basis for the Communists' international solidarity. Distinct from the ineradicable strife, as Lenin put it, between the interests of the exploiters who fight over profits, markets and spheres of influence, working people of all countries have no such contradictions; their interests and aspirations are the same. On the other hand, it is apparent that the more influential a Communist party is in its own country, the weightier can be its contribution to the struggle for the Communists' common goals on the international scene.

True, one sometimes hears questions: is proletarian internationalism still relevant, has it not become outdated? There are also those who are apprehensive lest the calls to strengthen internationalist bonds uniting the Communists signify a desire to recreate some organizational center.

Strange apprehensions. So far as is known, no one, nowhere has put forth the idea of creating such a center. As to proletarian internationalism, that is the solidarity of the working class, of the Communists of all countries in the struggle for common goals; their solidarity with the struggle of the peoples for national liberation and social progress; the voluntary cooperation of fraternal parties while strictly observing the equality and independence of each of them; we believe such comradely solidarity of which the Communists have been the standard-bearers for more than a hundred years still preserves all its great significance in our time. It was and remains the powerful and tested tool of the Communist parties and the working-class movement in general.

Incidentally, our common class adversary, the international bourgeoisie, demonstrates quite a few instances of international coordination of its actions in the struggle against the revolutionary forces. Wherever the exploitative system finds itself threatened, wherever the forces of national and social emancipation, then democratic forces gain the upper hand in the course of the struggle and imperialism makes literally frenzied attempts to coordinate its counterattacks. Many are the examples of this in our day both in Europe and Africa, and elsewhere. Today when the prospect of Communist participation in government is taking shape in some West European countries, reactionary quarters, particularly in the NATO camp, have unleashed a campaign of open pressure and interference in the internal affairs of the countries concerned. And please note, comrades, what it is that they rally against: against the results of general elections. So, there you are: the imperialist politicians who are so vociferous about democracy and freedom are actually prepared to tolerate the one and the other, only so long as they do not infringe their absolute power.

Given these circumstances it is particularly important that we collectively demonstrate here in this conference the readiness of our parties to make their contribution to the struggle for attaining the jointly outlined objectives.

There is one sphere of our cooperation which calls for special mention. What is meant is the pooling of efforts toward the generalization of revolutionary experience, the further development of the theory of scientific communism created by K. Marx, F. Engels and V. I. Lenin. Each party contributes to the development of revolutionary theory. This theory, as V. I. Lenin justly stressed, "grows out of the sum total of the revolutionary experience and the revolutionary thinking of all countries in the world."

The Communist movement, comrades, has accumulated truly great experience. This includes the experience of building socialism under most diverse conditions which demonstrates both its general regularities and the diversity of concrete forms, and the experience of defending the vital interests of the masses, of gathering revolutionary forces, of the struggle for socialism in countries with different levels of development. All this calls for analysis and generalization, all the more so since the experience of each fraternal party, apart from its inimitable specific features associated with national peculiarities, invariably contains common features which are of interest to our entire movement. Life too constantly adds something new to the development of objective sociopolitical and economic processes in individual countries and on the world scale and to the struggle for the attainment of our common goals.

Regarding with great attention the creative endeavor of our comrades in the Communist family, we proceed from the fact that practical experience alone can be the criterion of the correctness or, conversely, the erroneousness of these or other propositions. But even before practice pronounces its final verdict, there is the possibility and the need to examine these propositions in comradely debate through a broad comparison of the viewpoints and experience of different parties. As a result, both theory and practice obviously stand to gain; our common cause stands to gain.

One should think that multilateral meetings convened from time to time for purposes of mutual information and exchange of opinion on these or other outstanding political questions would also be useful.

Comrades, Communists do not shut themselves up within the shell of their own movement. They are always prepared for joint efforts with all those who cherish the cause of peace and the interests of the peoples. The Final Act of the European Conference created a good foundation for ensuring peace and security in Europe. But it will take not only the efforts by governments, but actions by the popular masses as well, to attain this goal and to make relaxation of tension irreversible and peace truly inviolable.

Everything must be done so that the popular masses clearly realize that their vital interests demand active support for the initiatives and actions aimed at strengthening peace, security and cooperation. This, in our view, is one of the Communists' paramount tasks today, one of the paramount tasks of each fraternal party and all of them together. We believe, comrades, that our conference can and must play a significant part in this noble cause.

Here at this meeting of European Communist parties, we naturally speak first of all about the situation in Europe. At the same time the draft of our document devotes much room to the interaction of the struggle for peace and social progress on this continent with the struggle for peace and social progress in other parts of the planet. And this is only natural. Socialism, as the creators of our teaching predicted, became an objective condition and imperative need for the further progress of mankind.

We are struggling for peace and security throughout the world. From this rostrum we ardently greet all the participants in the national-liberation movement and once again pledge our invariable support to their just struggle for the freedom, independence and progressive development of their countries.

The contribution of the peoples of Asia, Africa, and Latin America to peace and progress is undoubtedly growing. Socialism is already deeply rooted in many countries that have cast off the colonial yoke of imperialism and taken the road of free, independent development. A considerable role in international life is played by the non-aligned movement that is known to all of us.

The document of this conference, on which we have agreed, expresses the readiness of the Communists to promote the establishment of a new equitable economic order in the world. The struggle for equal political and economic relations and cooperation of the developed countries with former colonial and dependent countries, relations such as have long been established with them by the Socialist states, is an important part of our parties' common internationalist duty.

Comrades, respect for the views of every participant, the democratic and truly comradely atmosphere of the discussion, a broad comparison of the experiences of various parties, the friendly concern for the interests of partners, allowed us all to arrive at joint assessments and conclusions on a number of topical problems that are of tremendous significance today for the peoples of Europe and the whole world. We were able to elaborate an important document on these questions based on the principles of Marxism-Leninism.

I would like to stress that the CPSU [Communist Party of the Soviet Union] regards this document as binding on our party to vigorously and persistently struggle for attaining the goals collectively set forth by the Communists of Europe.

We are convinced that the results of our conference, which raised high the banner of unity of European Communists, will help to pool our efforts, to activate our joint struggle for the vital interests of working people, for democracy and socialism, for lasting peace in Europe.

I thank you, comrades, for your attention.

KISSINGER WARNS OF EUROCOMMUNIST GAINS [3]

Henry A. Kissinger warned . . . [on June 9, 1977] that the growing political strength of Communist parties in Western Europe posed a grave threat to the nature of the Western world and he urged concerted efforts to prevent Communist election victories in Italy, France and Spain.

The former secretary of state did not take direct issue with the more relaxed approach of the Carter Administration toward the Communist parties of Western Europe, which have been gaining in strength as they have increased their independence from the Soviet Union, but he seemed to press President Carter to broaden his concern over human rights to include concern over possible Communist victories at the polls.

Human rights is not an abstraction concerned only with judicial procedures and unrelated to basic questions of political and geopolitical structure [he said]. We cannot fail to reckon the setback to European freedom that will result if Communist minorities gain decisive influence in European politics; we must not close our eyes to the effect on freedom throughout the world if the global balance tips against the West. . . .

Mr. Kissinger's speech . . . [was given at] a conference on Italy and Western European communism . . . [held in Washington, D.C.] and sponsored by the American Enterprise Institute for Public Research and the Hoover Institution on War, Revolution and Peace.

In essence, Mr. Kissinger repeated at length the point he had often made as secretary of state—that if Communists were allowed to play significant roles in Western European

[3] Article entitled "Kissinger Warns of Gains by Communists in Europe," by Bernard Gwertzman, reporter. New York *Times.* p A 6. Je. 10, '77. © 1977 by The New York Times Company. Reprinted by permission.

governments, particularly in Italy, France or Spain, this could have long-term eroding effects on the entire Atlantic alliance.

During the [1976] election campaign, many Democrats criticized Mr. Kissinger's position on this question.

Mr. Carter said . . . [in May 1977] that the United States favored the election of non-Communists in Europe but "it's not up to us to tell other people how to vote or how to choose their leaders or who those leaders should be."

The effect of Mr. Carter's policy has been to leave the impression that the Administration was not overly concerned by the situation in Western Europe, some diplomats have said.

The Carter Administration has also eased visa policies, allowing, on a case-by-case basis, Western European Communists to visit this country when invited by American groups.

Mr. Kissinger, in his speech, said that there must be economic and social reforms in Europe to deprive the Communists of much of their appeal.

But in addition, he said, the United States must encourage "an attitude of resolve and conviction."

"We must frankly recognize the problem that we will face if the Communists come to power," he said. "We must avoid giving the impression that we consider Communist success a foregone conclusion by ostentatious association or consultation with Communist leaders or by ambiguous declarations.

"We do our friends in Europe no favor if we encourage the notion that the advent of Communists and their allies into power will make little or no difference to our own attitudes and politics," Mr. Kissinger said.

"If the United States has a responsibility to encourage political freedom throughout the world, we surely have a duty to leave no doubt about our convictions on an issue that is so central to the future of the Western alliance and therefore to the future of democracy," he said.

CARTER MOVES TO CHECK EUROCOMMUNISM [4]

"Being confident of our own future, we are now free of that inordinate fear of communism. . . ." That was President Carter's view of the world, especially of the European part of it, when he made a celebrated speech at Notre Dame University. However, Mr. Carter and his Administration have logged many miles since that day . . . [in] May [1977] in South Bend [Indiana]. In the interim the President's view of communism seems to have stiffened and Washington's once tacit acceptance of Eurocommunism has gone out the window.

On his recent visit to France [January 5-7, 1978] he took pains to caution the French Socialist leader, François Mitterrand, on the dangers of an alliance with the French Communist party. . . . [Early in January 1978] as Italy's Communist party was making yet one more vigorous bid for a larger share of the power, the State Department rushed home its ambassador for consultations and issued a statement urging Italians to try to reduce Communist influence in their political life.

Not that Prime Minister Giulio Andreotti and his Christian Democratic party needed urging. Ever since a brief period following World War II when Communists did participate in the government, the Christian Democrats have gone through political contortions to avoid repeating the experience. Even during Mr. Andreotti's latest term in office, during which he has governed only with the benign abstention of Enrico Berlinguer's Communists on crucial votes, the relationship has remained taut with mutual distrust.

So taut in fact that when . . . [in January 1978] the Communists, citing the woeful economic situation and a crescendo of terrorism, called for a "national emergency government" that would include Communists, Mr. Andre-

⁴ From article entitled "U.S. and Italy Move to Check Communists." New York *Times.* sec IV, p 1. Ja. 15, '78. © 1978 by The New York Times Company. Reprinted by permission.

otti and his colleagues refused. They did so even despite the near certainty of defeat in parliament. . . .

US DEFENSE AND SOVIET TIES [5]

Let me deal at the beginning with some myths.

One myth is that this country somehow is pulling back from protecting its interests and its friends around the world. That is not the case, as will be explained in this speech and demonstrated in our actions as a nation.

Another myth is that our defense budget is too burdensome and consumes an undue portion of our federal revenues. National defense is, of course, a large and important item of expenditures; but it represents only about 5 percent of our gross national product and consumes approximately one fourth of our current federal budget.

It also is a mistake to believe that our country's defense spending is mainly for intercontinental missiles or nuclear weapons. About 10 percent of our defense budget goes to strategic forces for nuclear deterrence. More than 50 percent of it is simply to pay and support the men and women in our armed forces.

Finally, some believe that because we possess nuclear weapons of great destructive power, we need do nothing more to guarantee our security. Unfortunately, it is not that simple. Our potential adversaries have now built up massive forces armed with conventional weapons—tanks, aircraft, infantry and mechanized units. Those forces could be used for political blackmail and could threaten our vital interests—unless we and our allies and friends have our own conventional military strength as a counterbalance.

National Communism and Intervention

Let us review how national security issues have changed over the past decade or two.

[5] From an address by President Jimmy Carter on US defense policy and policy toward the USSR, delivered March 17 at Wake Forest University, Winston-Salem, North Carolina. New York *Times*. p 9. Mr. 18, '78. © 1978 by The New York Times Company. Reprinted by permission.

The world has grown both more complex and more interdependent. There is now division among the Communist powers; the old colonial empires have fallen, and many new nations have risen in their place; old ideological labels have lost some of their meaning.

There have also been changes in the military balance among nations. Over the past twenty years the military forces of the Soviets have grown substantially—both in absolute numbers and in relation to our own. There also has been an ominous inclination on the part of the Soviet Union to use its military power to intervene in local conflicts with advisers, with equipment and with full logistical support and encouragement for mercenaries from other Communist countries, as we can observe today in Africa.

This increase in Soviet military power has been going on for a long time. Discounting inflation, since 1960 Soviet military spending has doubled, rising steadily by 3 to 4 percent every year, while our military budget is actually lower than it was in 1960.

The Soviets, who traditionally were not a significant naval power, now rank No. 2 in the world in naval forces.

In its balanced strategic nuclear capability the United States retains important advantages, but over the past decade the steady Soviet buildup has achieved functional equivalence in strategic forces with the United States.

These changes demand that we maintain adequate responses—diplomatic, economic and military.

Military Parity and Détente

We have recently completed a major reassessment of our national defense strategy, and out of this process have come some overall principles designed to preserve our national security during the years ahead.

☐ We will match, together with our allies and friends, any threatening power through a combination of military forces, political efforts and economic programs. We will not allow any other nation to gain military superiority over us.

☐ We shall seek the cooperation of the Soviet Union and other nations in reducing areas of tension. We do not desire to intervene militarily in the domestic affairs of other countries or to aggravate regional conflicts, and we shall oppose intervention by others.

☐ While assuring our military capabilities, we shall seek security through dependable, verifiable arms-control agreements where possible.

☐ We shall use our great economic, technological and diplomatic advantages to defend our interests and to promote our values. We are prepared, for instance, to cooperate with the Soviet Union toward common social, scientific and economic goals—but if they fail to demonstrate restraint in missile programs and other force levels and in the projection of Soviet or proxy forces into other lands and continents, then popular support in the United States for such cooperation will erode.

These principles mean that, even as we search for agreement on arms control, we will modernize our strategic systems and revitalize our conventional forces. We shall implement our policy in three ways:

☐ By maintaining strategic nuclear balance;

☐ By working closely with our NATO allies to strengthen and modernize our defenses in Europe; and

☐ By maintaining and developing forces to counter any threats to our allies and our vital interests in Asia, the Middle East and other regions of the world.

SALT

Our first and most fundamental concern is to prevent nuclear war. The horrors of nuclear conflict, and our desire to reduce the world's arsenals of fearsome nuclear weapons, do not free us from the need to analyze the situation objectively, and to make sensible choices about our purposes and means.

Our strategic forces must be—and must be known to be —a match for the capabilities of the Soviets. They must never be able to use their nuclear forces to threaten, coerce or blackmail us or our friends.

Our continuing major effort in the SALT [Strategic Arms Limitation Treaty] talks now under way in Geneva are one means toward the goal of strategic nuclear stability. We and the Soviets already have reached agreement on some basic points, although still others remain to be resolved.

We are not looking for a one-sided advantage, but before I sign a SALT agreement on behalf of the United States, I will make sure that it preserves the strategic balance, that we can independently verify Soviet compliance and that we will be at least as strong relative to the Soviet Union as we would be without an agreement.

But in addition to the limits and reductions of a SALT II agreement, we must take other steps to protect the strategic balance. During the next decade improvements in Soviet missiles can make our land-based missile forces increasingly vulnerable to a Soviet first strike. Such an attack would amount to national suicide for the Soviet Union, but, however remote, it is a threat against which we must constantly be on guard.

Rapid Effort on Cruise Missiles

We have a superb submarine fleet which is relatively invulnerable to attack, and we have under construction new Trident submarines and missiles which will give our submarine ballistic-missile force even greater range and security. I have ordered rapid development and deployment of cruise missiles to reinforce the strategic value of our bombers. We are working on the M-X intercontinental ballistic missile to give us more options to respond to Soviet strategic deployments. If it becomes necessary to guarantee the clear invulnerability of our strategic deterrent, I shall not hesitate to take actions for full-scale development and deployment of these systems.

Our strategic defense forces are a triad—land-based missiles, sea-based missiles and air-breathing systems such as bombers and cruise missiles.

Through the plans I have described, all three legs of the triad will be mechanized and improved. Each will retain the ability to impose devastating retaliation upon an aggressor.

The Defense of Europe

For thirty years and more we have been committed to the defense of Europe—bound by the knowledge that Western Europe's security is vital to our own. We continue to cooperate with our NATO allies in a strategy of flexible response, combining conventional and nuclear forces, so that no aggressor can threaten the territory or freedom which, in the past, we have fought together to defend.

For several years we and our allies have been trying to negotiate mutual and balanced reductions of military forces in Europe with the Soviets and the other Warsaw Pact nations, but in the meantime the Soviets have continued to increase and to modernize their forces beyond a level necessary for defense. In the face of this excessive Soviet buildup, we and our NATO allies have had to take important steps to cope with short-term vulnerabilities and to respond to long-term threats. We are significantly strengthening United States forces stationed in Western Europe and improving our ability to speed additional ground and air reinforcements to the defense of Europe in time of crisis.

International Alliances

For many years the United States has been a truly global power. Our longstanding concerns encompass our own security interests and those of our allies and friends beyond this hemisphere and Europe.

We have important historical responsibilities to enhance peace in East Asia, the Middle East, the Persian Gulf and in our own hemisphere. Our preference in all these areas is to turn first to international agreements that reduce the overall level of arms and minimize the threat of conflict. But we have the will, and we must also maintain the capacity, to honor our commitments and to protect our interests in these critical areas. In the Pacific we are protected, and so are our allies, by our mutual defense treaties with Australia, New Zealand, Japan and South Korea, and by our friendship and cooperation with other Pacific nations.

Japan and South Korea, closely linked with the United States, are located geographically where the vital interests of great powers converge. It is imperative that Northeast Asia remain stable. We will maintain and even enhance our military strength in this area, improving our air strength and reducing our ground forces, as the South Korean army continues to modernize and to increase its own capabilities.

In the Middle East and the region of the Indian Ocean we seek permanent peace and stability. The economic health and well-being of the United States, Western Europe and Japan depend upon continued access to oil from the Persian Gulf. In all these situations the primary responsibility for preserving peace and military stability rests with the countries of the region. We shall continue to work with our friends and allies to strengthen their ability to prevent threats to their interests and ours. In addition, however, we will maintain forces of our own which could be called upon if necessary to support mutual defense efforts.

The secretary of defense, at my direction, is improving and will maintain quickly deployable forces—air, land and sea—to defend our interests throughout the world. Arms-control agreements are a major goal as instruments of our national security, but this will be possible only if we maintain appropriate military force levels. Reaching balanced, verifiable agreements with our adversaries can limit the costs of security and reduce the risk of war. But even then, we must—and we will—proceed efficiently with whatever arms programs our security requires.

BIBLIOGRAPHY

An asterisk (*) preceding a reference indicates that the article or part of it has been reprinted in this book.

BOOKS, PAMPHLETS, AND DOCUMENTS

Bertsch, G. K. and Ganschow, T. W. Comparative communism; the Soviet, Chinese, and Yugoslav models. Freeman. '76.

Blackmer, D. L. M. and Tarrow, Sidney, eds. Communism in Italy and France. Princeton University Press. '76.

Brzezinski, Zbigniew, ed. Africa and the Communist world. Stanford University Press. '63.

Cammett, J. M. Antonio Gramsci and the origins of Italian communism. Stanford University Press. '67.

Carrillo, Santiago. Eurocommunism and the state. Lawrence Hill. '78.

Castro, Fidel. The Cuban revolution, national liberation, and the Soviet Union: two speeches by Fidel Castro. New Outlook. '74.

Cohen, L. J. and Shapiro, J. P. eds. Communist systems in comparative perspective. Anchor Press. '74.

Dallin, Alexander, and others, eds. Diversity in international communism; a documentary record, 1961-1963. Columbia University Press. '63.

Ionescu, Ghita. Comparative Communist politics. Humanities. '76.

Kazziha, W. W. Revolutionary transformation in the Arab world: Habash and his comrades from nationalism to Marxism. Knight. '75.

Klein, D. W. and Clark, A. B. Biographic dictionary of Chinese communism, 1921-1965. Harvard University Press. '71.

Kriegel, Annie. Eurocommunism: a new kind of communism? Hoover Institution Press. '78.

Lewis, J. W. ed. Peasant rebellion and Communist revolution in Asia. Stanford University Press. '74.

Logoreci, Anton. The Albanians; Europe's forgotten survivors. Gollancz. '77.

McInnes, Neil. Euro-communism. (Georgetown University Center for Strategics and International Studies. Washington papers v 4, no 37). Sage. '76.

Prpic, G. J. A century of world communism; a selective chronological outline. Barron. '74.

Revel, J. F. The totalitarian temptation; tr. by David Hapgood. Doubleday. '77.

Ro'i, Yaakov. From encroachment to involvement; a documented
study of Soviet policy in the Middle East, 1945-1973. Hal-
sted. '75.

Schapiro, L. B. ed. Political opposition in one-party states. Hal-
sted, '72.

Seton-Watson, Hugh. The imperialist revolutionaries: trends in
world communism in the 1960s and 1970s. Hoover Institution
Press. '78.

Staar, R. F. Communist regimes in Eastern Europe. 3d ed.
Hoover Institution Press. '77.

Staar, R. F. ed. Yearbook on international Communist affairs,
1977. Hoover Institution Press. '77.

Turner, R. F. Vietnamese communism: its origins and development. Hoover Institution Press. '75.
  Excerpts entitled: Communism in North and South Vietnam. Intellect.
  104:211. D. '75.

United States. Senate. Committee on Appropriations. A report on
West European Communist parties; June 1977. Supt. of Docs.
Washington, DC 20402. '77.
  Prepared by Foreign Affairs and National Defense Division. Congressional
  Research Service. Library of Congress.

Zasloff, J. J. and Brown, MacAlister, eds. Communism in Indochina; new perspectives. (Lexington Books) Heath. '75.

PERIODICALS

Annals of the American Academy of Political and Social Science.
432:96-109. Jl. '77. China's role in Africa. G. T. Yu.

Atlantic. 240:20+. Ag. '77 Reports and comment: Turin. God-
frey Hodgson.

Black Scholar. 6:41-51. My. '75. Socialism in Tanzania: a case
study. Horace Campbell.

Commentary. 62:25-30. Ag. '76. Eurocommunism and its friends.
Walter Laqueur.

*Commentary. 62:48-50. N. '76. Italian communism at home and
abroad: the new class. Mauro Lucentini.
  Discussion. Commentary. 63:20-2+. Mr. '77.

Commentary. 62:51-4. N. '76. Italian communism at home and
abroad: the Soviet connection. M. A. Ledeen.
  Discussion. Commentary. 63:20-2+. Mr. '77.

Commentary. 63:27-33. F. '77. Anglocommunism? Robert Moss.
  Reply: Nation. 224:298-300. Mr. 12, '77. Commentary sees red; the phantom
  "Anglocommunism." B. D. Nossiter.
  Discussion. Commentary. 63:6+. My. '77; 64:18-19. Jl. '77.

Commentary. 63:43-8. F. '77. Third world fantasies. Walter Laqueur.

Commentary. 63:53-7. My. '77. Europe breaks apart. M. A. Ledeen.

Commentary. 64:33-43. O. '77. Africa, Soviet imperialism and the retreat of American power [Angola]. Bayard Rustin and Carl Gershman.

Commentary. 64:37-41. D. '77. Europe: the specter of Finlandization. Walter Laqueur.

Commentary. 64:42-6. D. '77. Europe: The collapse of the Social Democrats. Stephen Haseler.

*Commentary. 64:53-7. O. '77. News about Eurocommunism. M. A. Ledeen.
  Discussion. Commentary. 65:20+. F. '78.

Commonweal. 103:322 My. 21, '76. New Vietnam.

Commonweal. 104:483-4. Ag. 5, '77. New kind of communism?

Current: 196:42-5. O. '77. Eurocommunism and detente. Arthur Schlesinger Jr.

Current History. 69:223-6+. D. '75. From feudalism to communism in Laos. Richard Butwell.

Current History. 69:232-5+. D. '75. Revolutionary government of Vietnam. D. G. Porter.

Current History. 70:101-6+. Mr. '76. Poland: the price of stability. R. F. Staar.

Current History. 71:153-7+. N. '76. Angola and Mozambique: intervention and revolution. T. H. Henriksen.

Current History. 73:54-8+. S. '77. Foreign policy of the People's Republic [China]. D. W. Klein.

*Current History. 73:105-8+. O. '77. Soviet policy in Europe. A. Z. Rubinstein.

Economist 258:32-3. Ja. 3, '76. Halfway to independence; but are they halfway to democracy too [Western European Communist parties]?

Editorial Research Reports. v 1, no 15:287-304. Ap. 23, '76. Western European communism. Yorick Blumenfeld.

Forbes. 115:49-50+. Ap. 15, '75. Comfortable Communists [Italy].

Foreign Affairs. 54:691-707. Jl. '76. Communist question in Italy. Sergio Segre.

*Foreign Affairs. 55:539-53. Ap. '77. Europeanization of communism? Charles Gati.

Foreign Affairs. 55:800-14. Jl. '77. Eurocommunism after Madrid. J. O. Goldsborough.

*Foreign Affairs. 56:295-305. Ja. '78. Myths of Eurocommunism. J. F. Revel.

*Fortune. 93:92-5+. F. '76. Communism's crisis of authority; world Communist movement. Daniel Seligman.

Fortune. 93:116-19+. Mr. '76. Communists in democratic clothing. Daniel Seligman.
  Same abr: Reader's Digest. 108:147-51. Je. '76.

Intellect. 104:563. My. '76. State of the world: Communist system: monolithic or diverse? L. H. Legters.

Intellect. 106:116-17. O. '77. Red scare in Moscow. R. H. Heindel.

Nation. 223:35-6. Jl. 17, '76. Brezhnev at bay; meeting of European Communists in East Berlin.

*Nation. 223:42-6. Jl. 17, '76. Report from Luanda: a new Angolan society. Kevin Brown.

*National Review. 26:755-7. Jl. 5, '74. Communism, Dalmatian style. James Burnham.

*National Review. 26:813-14. Jl. 19, '74. Communism or communisms [Yugoslavia]? James Burnham.
    Reply. National Review. 27:284. Mr. 14, '75. Can communism mellow [Yugoslavia]? S. M. Draskovich.

*National Review. 26:1094. S. 27, '74. Chilean lessons. James Burnham.

National Review. 27:377. Ap. 11, '75. Our stake in the Portuguese revolution; excerpt from statement, March 2, 1975. J. L. Buckley.

National Review. 27:1236-9. N. 7, '75. Coalition in Italy? Ernest Van Den Haag; C. B. Luce.
    Discussion. National Review. 27:1452-3. D. 19, '75.

National Review. 28:27. Ja. 23, '76. Nobody but us Democrats [Western Europe]. James Burnham.

National Review. 28:1395. D. 24, '76. International party; Leonid Brezhnev's goal. James Burnham.

National Review. 29:77. Ja. 21, '77. Soares on the trapeze [elections, Portugal].

*National Review. 29:83-6. Ja. 21, '77. Other Angola; UNITA. R. B. McColm and David Smith.

National Review. 29:258-63. Mr. 4, '77. Maoism is dead. F. B. Randall.

National Review. 29:351. Mr. 18, '77. When is a nation Marxist? W. F. Buckley Jr.

National Review. 29:425. Ap. 15, '77. Triple play [Africa].

National Review. 29:487-8. Ap. 29, '77. New Vietnam. L. T. Anh.

National Review. 29:556. My. 13, '77. Carrillo in sheep's clothing; Madrid summit. E. M. von Kuehnelt-Leddihn.

National Review. 29:769. Jl. 8, '77. Notes on Eurocommunism. James Burnham.

National Review. 29:816. Jl. 22, '77. Eurocommunism—two views.

National Review. 29:821. Jl. 22, '77. Picking the lock; French Eurocommunism. James Burnham.

National Review. 29:873. Ag. 5, '77. Some Euroquestions. James Burnham.

National Review. 29:1420. D. 9, '77. Carrillo 'neath the elms; speeches at Yale. Richard Brookhiser.

*New Republic. 172:4-5. My. 3, '75. Our SOBs; communism and the Vietnamese war. H. R. Isaacs.
    Same with title: U.S. policy and China. Current. 174:41-4. Jl. '75.

New Republic. 174:16-21. Ap. 3, '76. Italy's Russian sugar daddies. M. A. Ledeen and Claire Sterling.

New Republic. 177:8-9. Jl. 2, '77. Europe's future. M. A. Ledeen.

New Republic. 177:22-3. Ag. 6, '77. Kremlin cracks the whip [Spain, Western Europe]. M. A. Ledeen.

*New York Times. p A6. Je. 10, '77. Kissinger warns of gains by Communists in [Western] Europe. Bernard Gwerzman.

New York Times. p A27. Je. 10, '77. How Carter is handling Euro-communism. James Reston.

*New York Times. sec III, p 1+. D. 18, '77. The Cuban economy: how it works. Ann Crittenden.

New York Times. sec I, p 8. D. 25, '77. For a peaceful holiday in Poland, a full larder. D. A. Andelman.

New York Times. sec IV, p 1. D. 25, '77. Consumerism—a dirty word [USSR]. D. K. Shipler.

*New York Times. sec IV, p 4. D. 25, '77. East Europeans are better off. D. A. Andelman.

*New York Times. sec IV, p 1. Ja. 15, '78. U.S. and Italy move to check Communists.

New York Times. p E2. F. 12, '78. For many Somalis, it was a war that wasn't. John Darnton.

*New York Times. p E4. F. 12, '78. Berlinguer practices a guided democracy. Paul Hofmann.

New York Times. p E5. Mr. 5, '78. Yugoslavia's army, even divided, is the power. D. A. Andelman.

New York Times. p 1+. Mr. 18, '78. Moscow charges President is using threat, distortion. D. K. Shipler.

*New York Times. p 9. Mr. 18, '78. Excerpts from [President] Jimmy Carter's speech on defense policy and Soviet ties [given March 17].

New York Times Magazine. p 8-9+. Jl. 13, '75. Revolution of the red carnations [Portugal]. J. P. Davies.

New York Times Magazine. p 9-11+. Jl. 13, '75. I care nothing for elections, ha, ha! [interview ed. by Oriana Fallaci]. Alvaro Cunhal.

New York Times. p 1+. Jl. 31, '78. Albania sends China harsh note blaming Peking's slights for rift.

*New York Times Magazine. p 32-4+. Ap. 25, '76. Vietnamizing South Vietnam. Max Austerlitz (pseudonym).

New York Times Magazine. p 13+. My. 9, '76. Communism, Italian style. Alvin Shuster.

*New York Times Magazine. p 18-20+. F. 12, '78. Europe's reds: trouble for Moscow. Edward Crankshaw.

Orbis. 19:958-70. Fall '75. Revolutionary war in Southeast Asia. Robert Thompson.

Orbis. 21:29-43. Spring '77. Struggle for Mao and the future. R. A. Scalapino.

Senior Scholastic. 108:6-7. F. 10, '76. Angola . . . another Vietnam?

Senior Scholastic. 109:6-9+. Mr. 10, '77. Euro-communism.

Survey. 21:94-113. Summer '75. Rumania: background to autonomy. G. J. Gill.

Time. 104:48+. O. 7, '74. Twenty-five years of Chairman Mao [People's Republic (China)].

Time. 105:50-1. Mr. 31, '75. Italy: détente at the neighborhood level.

Time. 106:26-7. Jl. 28, '75. Red rule in Fiat city [Diego Novelli elected mayor of Turin].

Time. 106:22-7. Ag. 11, '75. Western Europe's first Communist country [Portugal]?

Time. 106:28. Ag. 11, '75. How the Communists survived [Portugal].

Time. 106:32. D. 8, '75. Europe's new renegade reds.

Time. 107:30-7. F. 16, '76. Slow road to socialism [Vietnam].

Time. 107:25-6. My. 31, '76. Communists seize the initiative [Italy].

Time. 108:54. D. 13, '76. Andreotti: *rebus sic stantibus* [Italy].

Time. 109:49. Je. 20, '77. Danger: Eurocommunism [views of Henry Kissinger].

Time. 110:19. Jl. 4, '77. Savaging a comrade; Russian attack on Spanish Communist party.

*Time. 110:32. Jl. 11, '77. Quotations from chairman Carrillo.
        Excerpts from *Eurocommunism and the state*, by Santiago Carrillo.

Time. 110:32-3. Jl. 11, '77. Eurocommunism: Moscow's problem too.

*Time. 110:33. Jl. 11, '77. Nearer the historic compromise [Italy].

*Time. 110:47-8. O. 3, '77. Big brawl in Bologna; students against Italian Communist party.

Time. 110.47. N. 21, '77. Apostle Carrillo.

*Time. 110:48. N. 28, '77. Russians, go home [Somalia]!

U.S. News & World Report. 78:60. Ap. 14, '75. Only 10 per cent of the people, but most of the power [Portugal].

U.S. News & World Report. 80:34-5. Mr. 22, '76. Revolt of West Europe's reds: alarm for Russia—and U.S. too. Joseph Fromm.

*U.S. News & World Report. 81:26-8. Jl. 5, '76. Global survey: where Communists are gaining—and losing—in bids for power.

U.S. News & World Report. 81:24-7. Ag. 9, '76. In next decade—breakup of Communist world?

*U.S. News & World Report. 81:66-8. N. 1, '76. What's causing the crack in the Communist monolith?

*U.S. News & World Report. 82:29-30+. Mr. 28, '77. Eyewitness account of life in Castro's Cuba. C. J. Migdail.

U.S. News & World Report. 83:28-30. Ag. 1, '77. Brezhnev's nightmare: breakaway in Europe.

U.S. News & World Report. 83:30-1. Ag. 1, '77. First-hand appraisal of Communist threat in Italy [interview, ed. by D. B. Richardson]. Giulio Andreotti.

U.S. News & World Report. 83:38-9. O. 17, '77. France: Communists spurn power? Joseph Fromm.

U.S. News & World Report. 83:51. O. 24, '77. Where the real power lies and the way it's exercised [Russia].

U.S. News & World Report. 84:59. Mr. 13, '78. At 85, Tito brings new worry to Carter White House.

*Vital Speeches of the Day. 42:610-16. Ag. 1, '76. European Communist parties; address, June 29, 1976. L. I. Brezhnev.

Vital Speeches of the day. 44:130-3. D. 15, '77. Canopy of tyranny; address, October 29, 1977. G. R. Ford.

Wall Street Journal. p 1+. Mr. 2, '76. Restrained reds [Florence, Italy]. Bowen Northrup.

Wall Street Journal. p 12. Ap. 2, '76. Western Europe and the Communists. Arthur Schlesinger Jr.

Wall Street Journal. p 12. Ag. 25, '77. Eurocommunism and détente [commentary on Henry Kissinger's address, June 9, 1977]. Arthur Schlesinger Jr.

World Today (London). 33:232-40. Je. '77. Social control in liberated Indochina. Dennis Duncanson.